Explaining the Parables

Explaining the Parables

Found in the Gospel of Luke

Robert Tippett

Copyright © 2020

All rights reserved. Produced in the United States of America. No part of this publication may be reproduced, or transmitted, in any form or by any means electronic, mechanical, photocopying, recording, or otherwise, without the prior written permission of the author.

ISBN 978-0-9801166-9-4 Paperback
ISBN 978-0-9801166-3-2 Epub

Published by Katrina Pearls, LLC

Dedication

This book is dedicated to the memory of my loving wife, who passed away in late 2019. Joycelyn Tippett was a fellow Apostle; my partner in service to God. She was the editor of my books and everything I have written since we married in 2006. She is greatly missed by a world that needs more like her. I am comforted by her continued spiritual presence with me and the insight to this series of books I owe to that presence.

Table of Contents

Foreword 9

Introduction 17

Lesson to Love Your Enemy 27

Parable of the Good Samaritan 67

Parable of the Prodigal Son 125

Parable of the Rich Man and Lazarus 173

Conclusion 217

Foreword

I have been called by God to write about Holy Scripture. I state that as a fact because I know it is the truth. Still, I fully realize that most people will doubt my claim. For them, it is important to understand that I do not claim that I have been called by God to write about Holy Scripture so I can be recognized as a celebrity or special person. While I feel most special by this call, without God I would have nothing of value to say. I make my claim as a way of giving credit to God. Therefore, I have been called by God to write about Holy Scripture so others (or someone else) will hear God calling to them (or him or her), to serve God and know their own truth of a personal calling.

I was first called after the tragedy of September 11, 2001. Prior to that, I had a casual interest in Nostradamus, owning one book that listed his prophecies, most of which made no sense to me. I was called to understand how to read his quatrains (4-line poems) for meaning. My understanding deepened as the years subsequently passed; but the clarity that has always remained was that Nostradamus was a prophet of God, who was called to write Holy Scripture in a divine language.

Parables Explained: Foreword

The language of Nostradamus was French (now termed Old French), of which I knew nothing. The one book I possessed about *The Prophecies* was an English translation, listed beside the French text. I found I was called to investigate the translations, which at the time was a tedious and painstaking process, which often led me to my own mistranslations, due to weak data sources. After finding a good Old French dictionary and the advent of Wiktionaire.com (which helped immensely on verb conjugations), I was able to do my own accurate translations. In this process I clearly saw that every English translation available in all books published about *The Prophecies* was paraphrased and not a literal reproduction of what was written.

By 2011, after a decade of continuous study and research into the French text and after obtaining replicas of the earliest publications of Nostradamus' work in Old French, I was about to publish a book entitled *The Systems of Nostradamus: Instructions for Making Sense of The Prophecies*. That work addresses how Nostradamus wrote in a divine syntax that utilized Old French as the base language, but all attempts to translate divine language utilizing the syntax of French would lead to errors and oversights of intended meaning.

In 2006, through my marriage to a woman that was Episcopalian, I returned to organized religion on a regular basis for the first time in forty years. As I sat in a church pew and heard (as I read along) the Episcopal Lectionary for each Sunday read aloud, I could see a strong similarity in the Scriptures of the Holy Bible and the writings of Nostradamus. Because I was growing in my insight about the Holy Scripture that I saw *The Prophecies* to be, I could see Nostradamus as a 'modern' prophet of God, reborn as

Jesus Christ (as are all Apostles), who all wrote in the same divine syntax. All the Holy Books were written in the same way: In a human language that was not properly translated, due to an inability to see the divine syntax that came from God.

My ability to discern meaning from *The Prophecies* of Nostradamus made it possible for me to use the same techniques and apply them to Biblical texts and gain deeper insights. Immediately, I was not hearing priests orate sermons that expressed the truth of meaning that was within the written words, due to the English translations (those read aloud) not encompassing the true depth the words contained. I then began a search for deeper insight from Bible study programs at various Episcopal churches my wife and I attended, with little advancement made. That led me to enroll in a thirty-five week course designed for educating the laypeople for ministry. That too yielded only more frustration. Everywhere I turned, what I would add to the group discussions was so unknown it was often rejected, simply because no scholar had written anything that said what I said (a parallel to the rejections I heard for posing a new concept on Nostradamus' prophecies).

This led my wife and I to attempt to make the insights that I was having (all from being led by God to follow inklings of thought to amazing discoveries) to promote articles written on a website, under the partnership we called Katrina Pearls. Our website was hosted by Yahoo and primarily was designed to promote Nostradamus as a prophet of Jesus Christ. Still, I also published many articles on a collection of topics on social media sites, between 2009 and 2012. The permanence of those postings was based on the sudden closure of websites that solicited a need for articles and my personal dissatisfaction with the webhosting service we paid to maintain.

By 2013, my writings about the meaning of *The Prophecies* of Nostradamus became secondary to a program I began, which was a three-year endeavor to write notes on all possible lectionary readings for each Sunday, with those notes leading to an overall sermon that connected all the threads of insight from Old Testament, Psalms, Epistles and Gospel readings chosen. In doing that, I could see the clerics who made that lectionary did so with divine insight. That program I produced was made available freely on a GoDaddy website, which I terminated in 2016. Eventually, the only place my writings were available (other than my self-published books) was on WordPress blogs I created, without promotion or advertisement.

On WordPress I created one blog that posted articles about Nostradamus. More relevant to where my focus had evolved (on Biblical interpretation), I created a blog named Our Daily Bread and then another entitled Bus Stop Sermons. Still, in all my postings (which were well more than what one would expect to find on a 'blog'), the number of clicks were low, with comments by readers seldom found. When I found all of my blogs only having clicks in Communist China, with many of my free articles listed found to be offered as available on dangerous websites that required personal information to gain access (including payments), I made all my postings unavailable for about six months. When I again made them accessible, the small interest that was once there had gone away.

It is this history of having produced much reading material that I deeply believe should be read by an audience that seeks to know more about Holy Scripture than is readily available (including priests and pastors searching for insight for their preparation of sermons) that I have decided to publish much of what has previously been available. Because I have so much written text that needs a serious audience, I have devised a plan to produce a series of books (including e-books), where each will focus on a limited number of articles.

In 2014 I published my first book that focused on Biblical interpretation. The title of that work is *The Cain & Abel Story*, which is deep insight applied to the fourth chapter of the Book of Genesis. That book is very short, relative to normal books, but at 126 pages shows how deep the analysis of Holy Scripture becomes. It is that depth of analysis that makes what I offer become too much for the casual reader of Christian 'fluff'.

My objective is to produce print books with a length of 200-250 pages. I plan to sort the articles into groupings that support one another in some way. Due to the depth of analysis, which is based on the original language being compared to the English paraphrases offered in churches on Sundays, I understand that only so much can be absorbed by a typical reader. Still, it is most important that this depth be exposed, so the reader does not come away with belief in what I write and instead comes away with a vision of the truth that is deeply personal. This will fulfill why God has called me to write about things I would otherwise have no ability to write about at all.

It is my hope and prayer that this planned series of books will open the eyes and hearts of readers on a broad scale, so the questions that have risen about Christianity can be answered. The Christian population has been dwindling significantly over the past fifty-plus years, due to many factors. The 'fire and brimstone' scare tactics have long worn too thin to work. The appeasement of criminals (the basest of sinners), by seeing moral laws as amoral, has opened the door to waves of acceptance-as-forgiveness, while persecuting those affected by crimes. The Roman Catholic Church has added fuel to this fire by protecting sexual predators disguised as shepherds. The politics of socialism has raised a cry against religion having any reason being in the development of governing rules. The children have left the churches of Christianity because their parents cannot answer properly the questions raised, while the parents have grown from rebellious children to become largely ignorant of Holy Scripture. For the most part, American Christians have the religious education level of a Sunday Schooler.

The churches have done little towards educating their congregations so they can eventually teach as they have been taught. No one is tested for the purpose of graduating into ministry, as grooming parishioners to leave the church seems to only guarantee a speedier demise. Elderly Christians still sit in pews listening to the sermons of priests and pastors, with an attitude that simply going to church is enough for eternal salvation. Many churches have split because of the politics at the lectern, where two opposing views of 'what Jesus would do' only further divides the flocks and poisons the brains of the religious-minded.

This series of books plans to open the souls of those who truly are interested in hearing answers to the whens, whats, wheres, hows and whys that Jesus taught. Those answers come from realizing the language of Holy Scripture is not English and not even simply Hebrew or Greek. The language written into the words of all Biblical authors is divine, as the Word of God. It is important that the truth is exposed, based on what the prophets have written.

The purpose of this series is to make it absolutely clear that Jesus did not come to have people ask, "What would Jesus do?" Instead, God sent him to ask everyone dying of mortal sin (regardless of human gender), "What will **you** do as My Son?" Once that is understood, then the issue ceases being about human beings judging the world and begins being totally about judging oneself.

Everyone who wishes to call oneself "Christian" must be resurrected as Jesus Christ, meaning true Christianity is (and has always been) about the self-sacrifice of egos and brain-led excuses and doubts, so one's souls can be baptized by the Holy Spirit. Upon that union between God and one's soul, together in one individual body of flesh, that body then serves the Father wholly, for as long as that body breathes. No longer are any excuses allowed for not doing the Lord's work, once one commits to a marriage to the Father; the consummation of that marriage being what brings about the rebirth of His Son in one's flesh. That is the beauty and truth of being <u>in the name of Jesus Christ</u>.

No one can control anyone other than oneself; but no one can control oneself without God's help. It is vital that that one see how that call has been made by God to all individuals who seek His help, through Holy Scripture. This series of books is designed to let that call be realized.

Parables Explained: Foreword

Introduction

I call this book "Explaining the Parables of Luke." As Jesus was the one telling the parables, Luke is then one who wrote of what Jesus taught through symbolism and metaphor. The word "parable" is defined as "a short fictitious story that illustrates a moral attitude or a religious principle." (Webster's) It is the "fictitious" part that creates confusion, because the central theme is placed on bringing understanding to stories taught by Jesus in ways that are not expressly stated. This makes a parable become like poetry, in the sense that the surface detail is difficult to set aside, in order to grasp the deeper meaning that exemplifies "a moral attitude or a religious principle."

When one is left to ponder the meaning behind poetic voice, which the parables of Jesus can be seen as, without the author explaining the meaning (directly or indirectly) the meaning becomes an opinion, a deduction, or a guess that may or may not be what was intended originally. In my work with the writings of Nostradamus, I found that his poems were read less with the poetic license that a poet is given through that medium of expression and more literally. The problem with that is a poetic voice is freed from the restrictions of normal syntax and normal definition, but a literal interpretation demands corrections to the written word to meet the mind's need for understanding; the creation of paraphrases that were not the whole intent.

Literal interpretations of Jesus' parables are how a fictitious story told seems to be exactly like the real stories of Jesus' ministry. A "certain man" in a parable is seen as one of the many people Jesus came in contact with, unlike how a fictitious story of a talking donkey would more readily demand one figure out why the author used an animal to represent humanity. Simply because Jesus told a story of a "certain man," it is difficult to see the metaphor of a "certain man" being Jesus. When Jesus is removed from the story told by Jesus, the parable is more difficult to understand.

Again, using my past work with Nostradamus' writings as valuable insight into how understanding the Holy Scriptures of the Bible demands both a whole view and a minute view (the macrocosm being a reflection of the microcosm and vice versa). Nostradamus wrote letters that explained the intent of his poems. Those letters (a preface and a letter sent to King Henry II of France) state the overall meaning of the nearly one thousand four-lined poems. The errors that are associated with the poetry of Nostradamus are not his, but the errors of interpreters who disregard his letters of instruction.

For instance, when the letters make it clear that the quatrains are of a distant future, to disregard that statement by the author as the intent (with the future being told poetically by God, through Nostradamus) and say, "These four lines of metaphor clearly point to the event that happened soon after Nostradamus published *The Prophecies*" is an error of reason. The fallacy comes from the limitations created by turning the fiction of a short story relative to a distant future into the literal of past and present events that surrounded the life of the poet author. The intent stated is ignored, making all interpretations that are not supported by the premise invalid, no matter how one part out of context seems to be something else.

In regard to the stories of Jesus' life and ministry that are found in the four Gospels, they read like a history lesson. That makes the four-sided view of Jesus as the Son of Man be read as a literal story of a certain man who was born, lived, preached and worked miracles, before being unjustly killed, only to resurrect from death, and stay around for a while longer before rising into heaven with the promise of returning. The limitations of that view keeps the reader from understanding that the four Gospels are telling a story that also will be found true in the distant future. It is most hard to see the Gospels as a parable that speaks as truly of our times today, and all times past, present and future, because the life of Jesus (as told by four different men) "illustrates a moral attitude" and "a religious principle."

This whole view of the minute details is then supported in the letters (called epistles) that were written by those who experienced the return of Jesus, by themselves likewise being filled with the Christ Spirit. The words written in the Epistles are then explaining the intent of the Gospels, just as Nostradamus wrote letters explaining the intent of his poems. The reason so many readily disregard what Nostradamus wrote in his letters is those letters are similarly difficult to discern, when normal syntax is applied (in his case, that of Old French). That complexity of writing style is perfectly mirrored in the writings of the Apostles, most particularly found in the complex writings of Paul.

Parables Explained: Introduction

All of the Apostles whose letters are part of the Holy Bible were writers that confirmed the story of Jesus, as told by the Apostles who wrote the four Gospels. Everything says the promise of Jesus returning was fulfilled the day after he Ascended into heaven (the Day of Pentecost). Christianity is the multiplicity of one who is and always will be "the Christ," known as Jesus. The Gospels tell of the one, which is a promise given to the distant future of the many that will be, who are now and who have been since then, reborn as Jesus Christ. The Apostles are the many who were so reborn; and the words of their letters explain what needs to be found conveyed in the stories of Jesus' life, including the parables he told.

Because this concept has been lost over time, it is important to see the truth of Holy Scripture bring this message back to the forefront of Christian consciousness. When Jesus said, "I have come to fulfill" the law and the prophets, that fulfillment must not be seen as ending two thousand years ago (give or take). The advent of Christianity, which spread rapidly for centuries, was the repetition of Jesus coming to fulfill the law and the prophets in those who were reborn in the name of Jesus Christ. They were not fulfillments of the law and the prophet by being simple believers that Jesus did that, but by being Jesus reborn, in possession of the same Christ Mind. That message is repeated over and over again in the Gospels and Epistles, but because it is hidden in the language (like a parable being told) it is easily not seen.

For the past decade I have been writing about the overlooked meaning found from scrutinizing the details of the original texts in the books of the Holy Bible. I have made reference after reference to the places where divine language needs to be applied for the meaning to surface and be known. Over the past decade my writings have surfaced and disappeared, due to the unstable and changing nature of the Internet and websites. What was here today was gone tomorrow, so I now feel a need to make my writings have permanence in publication as books. This is the first in a planned series of reproductions of past articles, with edits and additions making everything new again.

In this first book, I wanted to focus on parables told by Jesus, which I had deeply analyzed previously. As I searched through my files and looked for well-known stories that were commonly known by children, but still causing adults to ponder, I found two that were unique to Luke's Gospel. The two are recognized as The Parable of the Prodigal Son and The Parable of the Rich Man and Lazarus. In an attempt to find a third, which I would analyze here for the first time in public view, I wanted to find a meaty parable that was unique to Luke, with a caveat.

It is important to realize that Jesus spent four days travelling into Jerusalem to preach in parables publically, after his triumphant entrance there for his final Passover observance. I wanted to maintain a focus on the parables that only Luke reported, but prior to that time in Jesus' life. It was then that I decided to write about The Parable of the Good Samaritan, which I found surprising that I had never written about that (in-depth) before. That choice then raised another need.

The impetus that led to Jesus telling that parable was the question, "Who is my neighbor?" Because that question arose from the dawning that the Law was based on loving

Parables Explained: Introduction

God completely and loving one's neighbor as oneself, the modern misunderstanding of that need to "love" demanded that I also bring in the prior lesson that Jesus taught based on "love." That was his teaching that one should "love your enemies," which Jesus had stated prior to his telling of a good Samaritan.

Because of the depth required to discern The Parable of the Good Samaritan and the depth demanded to bring out the meaning of Jesus teaching his disciple to "love enemies," a separate article needed to be written. For as much as I had previously written about this issue of "love," I had not focused solely on the teaching found in Luke 6 (or that also recounted in Matthew 5). This means this book was set to focus on four writing from the Gospel of Luke, with a good deal of the contents being new material.

By narrowing the scope of this book to the lessons and parables of Jesus that were told before his final days in public ministry, the four articles in this book show how Jesus approached his ministry. First, he had to choose those who would be his closest followers, as those devoted to traveling with Jesus and providing for his needs. Chapters five and six of Luke's Gospel tells of Jesus calling his first disciples and then naming the twelve disciples that would act as his bishops.

It is in chapter six that we find the lesson to "love your enemies." This was Jesus preaching to the multitude, during his "sermon on the mount." Then, after Jesus had sent his twelve disciples out into a mini-ministry, John the Baptist was beheaded. This led to the feeding of five thousand and his eventual transfiguration, which was over more than a year's time. As Jesus' last year of ministry was well underway, he sent out seventy-two disciples in their mini-ministries, leading to his teaching those disciples the meaning of "love your neighbor as yourself" (found in chapter ten).

Then, with Jesus attracting large crowds and the careful watch of the Pharisees and scribes, we find Jesus being again confronted as a teacher that did not teach his disciples properly. This led to Jesus telling the parable about "a man with two sons," which has been termed The Parable of the Prodigal Son. This is actually the third of three metaphorical stories told to the Pharisees, all of which addressed something lost and then found. The entirety of Luke's fifteenth chapter tells those three parables.

Following that lesson being made, which at least some of the disciples who accompanied Jesus were present to hear, we find Jesus regularly teaching his disciples, with Luke mentioning briefly how a man who divorces his wife so he can marry another woman commits adultery. This can be intuited as from the time Matthew reported, as being told on the other side of the Jordan River when a Pharisee tested Jesus about the issue of divorce. From such a deduction, one can assume that Jesus told the parable about the rich man and Lazarus in a like setting, where some disciples were present at the time Jesus was confronted by one of the Temple's elite, who was reflected in the "rich man" of the parable.

This scope of Jesus' ministry, as reflected in this book as three parables and one associated lesson, is set up to establish a clear pattern of expectations set for all who would forever follow Jesus, in the name of Christ. The whole view of his ministry, as reported in the four Gospels, requires more than simple obedience to the commandments of Jesus (as repetitions of Mosaic Law). This is because the minute details of Jewish life during the times of Jesus made them incapable of clearly communicating how obedience was to take place. Thus, Jesus was a reflection of that innate inability to understand divine language, without having divine assistance.

For as many who know the surface knowledge that has been taught by Christian churches about loving enemies and neighbors, about the rich and the poor, and about the wayward and lost, none will confess that what I am presenting here is what they have been told to believe. Christianity cannot be seen as an easy religion to invest in, simply because all one has to do is say "I believe in Jesus Christ" and buy a cross icon of some kind. It cannot be a whisper campaign, where it is one whispering to another what to believe, based on what has been passed down the line. Christianity can only be true to God when one has been there, done that, and seen the truth firsthand.

The point of this book and all subsequent books in this planned series is then to present the old, the warm and fuzzy, and the familiar as the topic of discussion. From there, I will remove all the clutter and limiting errors of translation and show the truly interested and honestly invested Christians (and anyone else) what is truly stated in Holy Scripture. This series then becomes an exercise in learning to master a new language, one that has divine origins. Once that language is mastered and one has established fluency, anything I have to say about anything found in the Holy Bible will be easily understood. At that point, the student will say, "But teacher, you forgot to mention all these other things that are there too."

That becomes an explanation about how John could end his Gospel by stating, "Jesus performed many other signs in the presence of his disciples, which are not recorded in this book. But these are written that you may believe that Jesus is the Messiah, the Son of God, and that by believing you may have life in his name." (John 20:30-31, NIV translation)

It is in that way that Jesus teaching his disciples and preaching to those who challenged his authority was done in mysterious words. Because the Temple elite thought they knew much more than Jesus, based on worldly measuring sticks, their questions and challenges were answered by other questions and nebulous answers. The parables seemed clear, but none of the depth of truth was grasped. The disciples, once risen to the state of Apostlehood, understood all that they had missed when students of Jesus. The rulers of Jerusalem never realized that truth.

This means the confusion of parables become Jesus speaking in a divine language that mirrored the imperfect state of mortal being his listeners owned. The words Jesus spoke act as a measuring stick that determines the living with the dead. Just as Jesus spoke in terms that had his students asking for clarification in private, so too did the Apostles write letters that brings scholars to their knees trying to understand their words.

The answers to all Christianity's questions can only come from one being able to see for oneself the truth. The truth is there to be had, but it requires effort that demonstrates belief, while setting the expectations of faith, with prayers for guidance to understanding. For that sight to come to one, one must prove a desire to learn the truth and demonstrate a willingness to work to gain the truth. That is the intent behind this book and all to come like it. The more effort one gives, the more divine inspiration will be the reward.

The Lesson to Love Your Enemies

Luke 6:27-36

In today's world where religion has become weakened by ignorance, there are many who still use religion as a weapon that can be used against others. History tells us this is nothing new, as the advent of Christianity and the growth of the Holy Roman Empire as the administrator of that religion has grown hatred (overt and cloaked) between the three religions said to worship the same God (by different names). What is less obvious is the war between the denominations of Christianity, which have been increasingly pronounced since the philosophical revolution commonly called the Age of Reason.

The mushroom that began with the disillusionment with the Church of Rome, splintering into a Church of England, followed by the Reformation spurred by Martin Luther, led to an openness to the belief that all human beings are equal, as opposed to the belief prior that most people were common and only special people (those related to God physically or spiritually) were chosen by God to lead the commoners. This gave rise to democracies, where royalty (mostly kings) surrendered power to philosophical governments, with those governments being separate and equal powers to the Church of Rome and/or its equivalents.

Parables Explained: The Lesson to Love Your Enemies

Since then, especially after the United States of America was founded totally on the principles of governmental rule without direct oversight by royalty or Church, and then the violent overthrow of France's royal rulers, the world of Christianity has slid down the slippery slope of ruin. It is headless now, which means the true wisdom of Scripture has been replaced by ideas and concepts that are crude mistranslations and misinterpretations of the New Testament teachings, designed to suit the agendas of politicians and philosophers. A perfect example of that mutation is the promotion of "love" as the remedy to all ills, using the words of Jesus as the reason to surrender whatever remains true Christianity has to the corruption of those who are, historically speaking, still at war with religions and want them all dead and gone.

In different places in the New Testament books, Jesus was remembered to have said, "Love one another," "Love your neighbors as yourself," and "Love your enemies." Besides completely misunderstanding the true meaning of "love," which cannot possibly be a human emotion that changes like a weather vane in the winds of human life, it absolutely forgets that "one another, neighbors, and enemies" are, and always will be, fixed entities of different states of being. While the false shepherds are crying out for Christians to sacrifice for everyone, based on "love," they have dissolved three into a meaningless one, thereby confusing "love" as being proved by obedience to the false shepherds.

In order to help clarify this confusion, I will present two of the messages presented by Jesus in Luke's Gospel, dealing with "enemies" and "neighbors." The passages are Luke 6:27-36, which is commonly referred to as Jesus speaking about "Love for Enemies," and Luke 10:25-37, which is commonly called "The Parable of the Good Samaritan." The New International Versions (NIV) of each reading is as follows:

Luke 6:27-36

> "But to you who are listening I say: Love your enemies, do good to those who hate you, bless those who curse you, pray for those who mistreat you. If someone slaps you on one cheek, turn to them the other also. If someone takes your coat, do not withhold your shirt from them. Give to everyone who asks you, and if anyone takes what belongs to you, do not demand it back. Do to others as you would have them do to you. If you love those who love you, what credit is that to you? Even sinners love those who love them. And if you do good to those who are good to you, what credit is that to you? Even sinners do that. And if you lend to those from whom you expect repayment, what credit is that to you? Even sinners lend to sinners, expecting to be repaid in full. But love your enemies, do good to them, and lend to them without expecting to get anything back. Then your reward will be great, and you will be children of the Most High, because he is kind to the ungrateful and wicked. Be merciful, just as your Father is merciful."

Luke 10:25-37

> On one occasion an expert in the law stood up to test Jesus. Teacher," he asked, "what must I do to inherit eternal life?" "What is written in

Parables Explained: The Lesson to Love Your Enemies

the Law?" he replied. "How do you read it?" He answered, "'Love the Lord your God with all your heart and with all your soul and with all your strength and with all your mind'; and, 'Love your neighbor as yourself.'" "You have answered correctly," Jesus replied. "Do this and you will live." But he wanted to justify himself, so he asked Jesus, "And who is my neighbor?" In reply Jesus said: "A man was going down from Jerusalem to Jericho, when he was attacked by robbers. They stripped him of his clothes, beat him and went away, leaving him half dead. A priest happened to be going down the same road, and when he saw the man, he passed by on the other side. So too, a Levite, when he came to the place and saw him, passed by on the other side. But a Samaritan, as he traveled, came where the man was; and when he saw him, he took pity on him. He went to him and bandaged his wounds, pouring on oil and wine. Then he put the man on his own donkey, brought him to an inn and took care of him. The next day he took out two denarii[e] and gave them to the innkeeper. 'Look after him,' he said, 'and when I return, I will reimburse you for any extra expense you may have.' "Which of these three do you think was a neighbor to the man who fell into the hands of robbers?" The expert in the law replied, "The one who had mercy on him." Jesus told him, "Go and do likewise."'

These two teachings of Jesus should be recognized as told on separate occasions. Still, as everything said by Jesus was the Word of his Father, spoken through the Son, they have to be recognized as the truth of Scripture, such that truth is consistent through all times. Therefore, what is said at one time can never alter that message when some similar truth is told. Nothing can be seen as contradictory; due to everything documented as said by Jesus is the absolute truth.

With this acceptance of the truth being told, knowing God spoke through the Son, Scripture has deeper meaning than what can be readily obtained from casual viewing. Each word spoken is the truth from God and cannot be dismissed. This is a common mistake of translations. While the concepts of loving enemies and loving neighbors can be gleaned from quickly reading these two passages, the truth that waits hidden, requiring God's assistance in understanding, means careful study of the Greek text. That is what this presentation will focus on doing, in order to uncover the truth of "enemies" and "neighbors," as two separate entities that cannot become other than those titles state.

Before delving deeply into Luke 6:27-36 it is important to know what was written prior to this statement about loving one's enemies. Verses 17 to 26 address blessing upon the disciples who followed Jesus (20-22) and woes promised to those who persecuted those who were truly devoted to God. In verse 22 Jesus said:

> "Blessed are you when people hate you, when they exclude you and insult you and reject your name as evil, because of the Son of Man."

As can be clearly seen from this translation of this unseen verse (when looking only at those verses dealing with "love your enemies"), Jesus has identified "enemies" as those who persecute God's followers. Therefore, it is their hatred that becomes a blessing for the "poor, hungry, and sorrowful" (seen in spiritual terms, not materially). Jesus was putting his spin on the words of the prophet Amos when he said "woe to the rich, satiated, and happy" (here, seen in material terms, not spiritual), as karmic debt is being built each and every day by one's actions towards others. As they say, "Payback is Hell."

With this background realized, one can then understand the first work of verse 27 is the capitalized connective word of exception, "*Alla*," which is translated as "But," while also meaning "On the other hand, However, or But instead." The capitalization is not to be overlooked, as it comes from a prophet's hand, led to write a capital "A" with purpose. The capitalization then says there is redemption to be had by changing one's course and turning from selfish ways ("enemy") to one that serves God completely.

Jesus then identified that exception as being "to you who are listening," or "hearing," or [most importantly] "to you who are comprehending" what Jesus' words say. Simply hearing Jesus talk is not the same as knowing what Jesus was talking about. That knowing comes from the insights of God, via His Holy Spirit. Jesus had the Holy Spirit within him, and his disciples had been touched by his divinity, named as apostles not long before. Even though they (sans Judas Iscariot) would not deeply understand until later (after Jesus died, resurrected, and ascended), they were opening their hearts as the words of Jesus hit their ears. Thus, the root Greek word that is translated as "hearing" ("*akouó*") figuratively means (according to HELPS Word-studies), "to hear God's voice which prompts Him to birth faith within." Redemption is possible to all who come to hear God's voice within.

It is then with that premise stated, of a follower of Jesus having become filled with the Holy Spirit, that the first word spoken by Jesus is "*Agapate*," a capitalized word meaning "Love." That word is spoken in the second-person plural present active voice, in the indicative, subjunctive, and imperative mood, meaning it is directed to the group of followers known as Christians, as a current act of "Love." The root verb "*agapaó*" means "to love" (Strong's definition) but also an act of "love, wish well to, take pleasure in, long for; denotes the love of reason, esteem." (Strong's usage) HELPS Word-studies adds the use in the Holy Bible implies "for the believer, preferring to 'live through Christ', i.e. embracing God's will (choosing His choices) and obeying them through His power." The capitalization places that deduction as the powerful intent behind the word spoken by Jesus, meaning it is not a statement to find it within one's human will to emotionally enjoy others, including wanting to touch and feel them sexually. "Love" is a statement of God's presence within those who follow in the name of Jesus Christ.

When the capitalization of "*Agapate*" is seen to stand on its own merit, as a statement of God's love within one's soul (Baptism by the Holy Spirit, thus not an ordinary sinful human being), the consequence will always mean one's righteousness (which is not a personal decision or self-willed state of being) will create in others a natural dislike. This then brings one to realize "the enemies of you" (from the Greek words "*tous echthrous hymōn*"). This is a very important concept to firmly grasp.

Parables Explained: The Lesson to Love Your Enemies

In the commonly viewed statement, "Love your enemies," the translation of "your" comes from "Love" having been stated in the second-person plural. This then makes that translation appear to be Jesus commanding his followers to treat their foes with acceptance, forgiveness, and to offer blessings as a way to smooth over all the rough edges that one's "enemies" have. When one changes the same words spoken (written by Luke) to say, "Your Love [will attract] to you the enemies," it ceases being a command and becomes a statement of truth. After all, Jesus did not come to change the Law, but to fulfill it." Therefore, Jesus was not commanding anyone to do anything different than God had passed along through Moses and the prophets.

This makes understanding the word spoken by Jesus, "*echthrous*," which is translated as "enemies." The word actually means, "hostile" (Strong's definition), but it implies "hated," which makes the word become a substitute for "enemy." (Strong's usage) The root word, "*exthrós*," means "someone openly hostile (at enmity), animated by deep-seated hatred," implying "irreconcilable hostility, proceeding out of a "personal" hatred bent on inflicting harm." (HELPS Word-studies) This understanding of what Jesus was calling the natural "enemies" of his followers (Christians), because they were filled with the Holy Spirit of God, says "enemies" are the worshippers of sin, who bow down before other gods (in particular Satan), as the opposites of "Love." In dualistic terms, this means "Love" is like the head side of a coin and "enemies" are like the tail side, such that the two sides will always be opposite and contrary of one another, due to "enemies" not being filled with the "Love" of God.

According to the NIV translation, verse 27 then goes on to

state, "do good to those who hate you." This also appears as Jesus giving a command to treat one's enemies differently that one's friends and neighbors. Instead, the literal translation form the Greek says, "good do to those hating you." In that ordering of the words, it is "good" (from the Greek word "*kalōs*") that comes first, followed by the action of "doing" (from the Greek word "*poieite*"), meaning to "do good" leaves it up to the individual to come up with ideas for how to act in ways determined to be "good." This demands one understand those two words spoken by Jesus.

The Greek word "*kalós*" better translates as "well" (Strong's definition), where its usage implies acts done "nobly, honorably, and rightly." (Strong's usage) This makes "good" simply be the opposite of "bad," which is then a statement that "Love" is seen through acts that are "upright, blameless, beautiful, fit, and commendable." (Synonyms from Thayer's Greek Lexicon) The root word of "*poieite*" ("*poieó*") does mean "do," but also is a word that states "I manufacture, construct, produce, cause, and form." This is then less a command to take the responsibility of "goodness" (a.k.a "righteousness") upon one's shoulders alone, and more a statement that God's "Love" is what "builds" or "makes" one become that character, in the face of "enemies."

This means Jesus was not telling someone to go and do good things to those who hate you. Instead, it is a statement that having been "made good" by God will give one the strength of construction to withstand whatever comes "from those who hate you." This accepts the certainty that a true Christian will face persecution in the name of Jesus Christ, but it is that state of being (where one has been reborn as Jesus Christ by God's "Love") that keeps one

Parables Explained: The Lesson to Love Your Enemies

"doing good."

Verse 28 then has Jesus recommending, "bless those who curse you, pray for those who mistreat you." The two operative words in those two separated word segments are then the first words of each: "bless" and "pray." In my mind, a word like "bless" is not something capable of a human being, even though it is regularly uttered by people pretending to be pious and priestly. For a priest (including an official bishop and even a pope) to make hand and finger motions, while saying, "Bless you" the implication is a human being saying "You have been blessed by me," which is sacrilegious. Prayer, on the other hand, is easily understood as a communication between a believer and God, as a petition for help. Confusion then comes from pronouncing one who curses as forgiven, while then praying for them as sinners being contradictory. This makes "bless" and "pray" seem to be opposites, rather than similar approaches in the face of hatred.

The Greek word spoken by Jesus that has been translated as "bless" is "*eulogeite*." It is a form of the root verb "*eulogeó*," which means, "to speak well of, praise" (Strong's definition), while being used to denote "I speak well of." (Strong's usage) HELPS Word-studies says the proper use is "to speak (reason) which confers benefit; hence, bless," adding the action of the word is to "confer what is beneficial." This uncovers the true reason behind a priestly "blessing," as it is not a hand motion that blesses, but the message that has been conveyed through a prophet from God. When prayer is understood as a form of communication to God for help, this understanding of "bless" means the prayers are answered by God through the voices of God's "Beloved ones."

This means Jesus was telling his disciples (and all future disciples of the Christ Mind) to continue speaking the truth to one's enemies, sent by God's Holy Spirit, regardless of the "curses" that flow from the mouths of the wicked. The use of the Greek word "*katarōmenous*," meaning "cursing," should then be seen as attempts made by the "enemies" of God to bring doom or evil upon those who serve God. To give in to those "curses" means to become just as evil as their souls are, which means they attempt to get the righteous to turn away from God. That is the intent of their words; so the response to that evil spoken by "enemies" is to preach the truth at all times.

This says there will be confrontations with one's "enemies," as they will be the ones who come to "curse" and defile. The Gospels place focus on how this played out in Jesus' life, where he constantly confronted his "enemies," when they came to him and sought to entrap him. Jesus did not go out of his way to seek the vile and venom that always comes from such poisonous snakes of humanity. He did not shy away either. Jesus always spoke the truth to his combative "enemies," which always had the effect of shutting their evil mouths, leading them to walk away from a confrontation they had lost. The truth always overcomes lies and exposes evils. Therefore, "prayer" is for those times when one's enemies have gone back into hiding.

The Greek word "*epēreazontōn*" was spoken by Jesus, which is translated as "mistreating." The root verb "*epéreazó*" means, "to revile" (Strong's definition), with the intent of usage being "I insult, treat wrongfully, molest, revile." (Strong's usage) The use of this word then states that one knows one's "enemies" are still those who "insult,

Parables Explained: The Lesson to Love Your Enemies

treat wrongfully, molest and revile" anyone who speaks the truth. Simply by speaking the truth when confronted by evildoers does not 'convert' "enemies" into friends. By realizing that fact, "prayer" becomes the way one asks God for the strength and courage to continue serving God, despite those who plot to bring ruin upon God's Apostles. The use of "prayer" is not so that others will be 'cured of their illnesses,' but for God's continued help in a world that is the only place where sin can thrive.

In verse 29, Jesus then set forth two scenarios that read as what to do "if something happens to one, brought on by a hater. We read the NIV translation as: "If someone slaps you on one cheek, turn to them the other also. If someone takes your coat, do not withhold your shirt from them." Basically, those two [two is always a number of duality] scenarios are statements about the material world, where the soul's possession is the body and the body's possessions are things, such as shirts and coats. It should then be realized that Jesus was saying, in effect, "Do not fight for worldly things, and maintaining possession of things of the earth will only keep one on that lower plane, not heaven. Still, there is deeper meaning found in Jesus' use of "cheek" and "coat" need to be understood.

First, the Greek word "*siagona*" translates as "Jaw" or "jawbone," but implies the "cheek." Both the jaw and the cheek are parts of one's head, which does much to project one's face. By seeing how a follower of Jesus has two cheeks, so if one side of the face is stuck, then let the other side be struck also, this misses the duality of a follower of Jesus, as one filled with God's Holy Spirit. The word "cheek" is then synonymous with the dual faces one wears when in the name of Christ. The one face is that of one's flesh, which is what one looks like to others. When people figuratively strike any follower of Jesus (in whatever manner, beyond slapping), the natural response is to strike back. Striking back relates to this passage from Leviticus, chapter 24:

> "Whoever takes a human life shall surely be put to death. Whoever takes an animal's life shall make it good, life for life. If anyone injures his neighbor, as he has done it shall be done to him, fracture for fracture, eye for eye, tooth for tooth; whatever injury he has given a person shall be given to him. Whoever kills an animal shall make it good, and whoever kills a person shall be put to death. You shall have the same rule for the sojourner and for the native, for I am the Lord your God." (Leviticus 24:17-22)

Knowing this legal right given to the priests of God (His Levites), it does not extend beyond those who are deemed "neighbors" (Hebrew "*hamitow*," from "*amith*"). A "neighbor" is different from an "enemy," thus Jesus was saying "enemies" must be dealt with differently. He was not sent to change the Law, but to fulfill it. Therefore, turning the other cheek does not mean an "enemy" is beyond deserving equal punishment for evil acts upon humanity [an eye for an eye], as it means a second face should instead be shown to evildoers.

This reverts to the First Commandment, which is commonly known as saying, "Thou shall have no other gods before me." In reality, based on the literal translation of the Hebrew, the First Commandment means, "Thou shall wear the face of no other gods before me." This is found in the

Parables Explained: The Lesson to Love Your Enemies

Hebrew word "*panaya*" means "face," but has mistakenly been translated as "me." The use of "*elohim*" as the plural number of "gods" [besides assuring the reader that there are indeed many lower-"g" gods] says that to be one devoted to YHWH via Covenant, one must stop seeing one's own face as a "god," or God will not show His face around that person. As such, Jesus followers not only wear their own human faces on top of their heads, but they also wear the face of God before them, as the Christ (in the name of Jesus). Therefore, the "other cheek" is the face of God, as Jesus Christ reborn; this must be the response to all attacks by haters.

[For all the world's pacifists who love to put on the face of self-ego and speak for Jesus *carte blanche*, keep in mind that is breaking the First Commandment. Also realize that the God of the Old Testament will do the striking back to all haters, so nothing deserving punishment will ever go unpunished. Jesus died on the cross at the hands of Jerusalem's Temple Jews and the Roman Empire; but Jesus lives and those great powers have been destroyed.]

Second, the Greek word "*himation*" is translated as "coat," but it better translates as "cloak." The word that is translated as "shirt" ("*chitōna*"), which follows as what should be offered after a demand for an outer garment, is again a statement of two layers of clothing. If one layer is taken away or removed, then also give up that covering left remaining. In regards to why Jesus specifically used "cloak" and "tunic" as articles of clothing that would be "taken away" or "given" in response to a taking, they reflect the holy garments worn by God's priests. This then is a statement that the true followers of Jesus, as servants of Yahweh, will not fight for robes or other priestly clothing, as the robes do not make the priest. A true priest stands naked before the Lord, owning none of its knowledge to schools, books, or sermons heard by people who love pomp and circumstance. That says the "enemies" are not always found in militaries of threatening nations, but in the churches and synagogues that profess to serve the One God.

Verse 30 then has Jesus adding, "Give to everyone who asks you, and if anyone takes what belongs to you, do not demand it back." In this translation the word "Give" is capitalized, such that important focus is placed on the act of "giving." In the Greek text, the word "*didou*" is written, where the lower-case spelling means, "to give, offer, grant, supply, and deliver." The importance is then taken away from that being a self-motivated act of "giving," but the word takes on importance by the Greek text surrounding that one word with comma marks, setting it as a one-word statement of what God expects His priests to do. That importance can then be seen as relative to "everyone asking" [a statement that Christianity would be open to Gentiles, who had been seen by the Temple Jews with great animosity].

Following the separation of "give" is the Greek word "*kai*," which acts as a marker to pay close attention to what is written next. This word, as a Divine utterance, is never to be taken as a simple conjunction or a 'oh by the way' additional remark. The word "*kai*" is God's way of calling attention (like one-word statements set off by comma marks) to His Word. The word "*kai*" then introduces the reader to a literal Greek statement that says: "from the [one] taking away what [is] yours."

The Greek word "*tou*" is a common masculine, singular,

neuter genitive form of *"ho"* (as an article), but can also be a pronoun, in all genders, as a form of *"tis."* This, like *"kai,"* appears to be an often repeated word of little significance, other than being a statement of the singular number. Above, I have shown it in translation as "the [one]." However, based on the scholastic translations of the Holy Bible that often calls for intuited meaning to come from simple words (done by the NASB), this word could imply "a condition" that is relative to all gifts being mandatorily "taken away." In that case, Jesus was establishing reasoning behind righteous giving, where what a priest of God "gives" is meant to be "taken away." This becomes an especially valid expectation when one comes to a priest asking for spiritual guidance. There is nothing that limits the word "give" to material riches or donations of wealth.

This then means that the one "taking away" a "gift," sent by God through a priest, should "not ask back." When the Greek word written is examined closely, *"apaitei"* says, "ask what is my due" or "demand back." To have this word preceded by the negative word "not" (*"mē"*), it is most important to see how Jesus is stating in verse 30 what it takes to be a true priest of God, which was not being found the case in Jerusalem's Temple. The same sense of expectation - to get something in return for preaching God's Word – goes on today. The cost of being a faithful servant of God is more than the value of amounts of silver, gold, copper, or paper dollars. Sacrifice of self in subjection to the Christ Mind is the demand, with faith being set in the Father to continue giving. Therefore, a true priest of the Lord (as Jesu most definitely was) does not pass around an offering plate after a sermon, setting forth an expectation to pay for what was supposed to be freely given.

Verse 31 then follows and is one of the most often quotes made by those who want their opinions be freely given, but with hidden expectation. It is, according to the NIV, "Do to others as you would have them do to you." This, of course, is a liberal translation that masks the whole truth that be told.

The Greek text slows this statement down, breaking it into two segments, separated by a comma mark (not found in the NIV translation). It also begins with the word "kai," setting the reader's attention to the importance that follows (again not found in the NIV translation). The Greek text is then: "*kathōs thelete hina poiōsin hymin hoi anthrōpoi , poieite autois homoiōs*," which literally translates (maintaining the order of the word written) as: "according to the manner in which you are willing that should do to you condition those of the human race , should do to them likewise." The break in these segments of words forces one to examine oneself first, where self-examination reveals oneself to be just as likely to have the same emotions and feelings as any other human being on the planet. From that self-awareness, as a human being, one should then act humanely to others. There is no motivation set forth by Jesus as to what expectations one should establish relative to how others will act in response. It simply, yet powerfully says, "You are judged by God based on your actions, not by the actions of others towards you."

This becomes a definition of "Love," as given to an Apostle. It means that "Love" is not an emotion but the insight that comes from the Christ Mind. It says that self-ego is what keeps one from experiencing God's "Love," such that selfish acts are made by those who blind themselves from seeing how their selfish actions done against others would be realized, if the same acts were done against them by others. It makes the antithesis of "Love" become, "Do unto others before they do unto you," which keeps the world in a state of hatred for anyone who is not committed to serving oneself – the center of everyone's world.

Law based on the Old Testament was a decree written down (eventually) on scrolls, which were memorized by the Israelites. The Laws of Moses was not governmental laws that every nation was committed to follow. They were external orders that God set in place, based on His "Love." The Laws were to be fulfilled by the onset of Jesus and Christianity, whereupon the Laws would be written into the hearts of the Apostles, such that "Love" would result in individuals who were committed servants of the Lord "would be willing to listen to God's insight as to the conditions of human existence" and act accordingly in one's actions. Those actions would be according to the Laws of "Love."

In Christian nations that have surfaced in the two thousand plus years after God sent His Son to fulfill that "Love," and spread God's "Love" to true Christians, those nations have incorporated the Laws of Moses (in particular the Ten Commandments) into their civil laws. Certainly, the laws of man are far from being capable of understanding the Divine Word the Laws of Moses contained. Mistranslations have led to misunderstandings and misunderstandings have created open debates as to the meaning of God's Laws. This means the understanding of that Law, as seen in human laws, has changed over time. This is particularly evident in the debates and arguments against the death penalty and defining "cruel and unusual punishment," such that any corporeal punishment (including the death penalty) is said to go against the teachings of Jesus (ignoring his claim, "I have not come to change the Law"). "Do unto others as you would have them do unto you" has become a motto for the persecution of those affected by heinous crimes, while the guilty face nothing akin to law in Leviticus – "an eye for an eye."

It must be held firmly that Jesus spoke in the plural number while expecting each one of the whole would be the same, as each being filled with God's Holy Spirit. If the whole world were to become filled with God's "Love," then there would be no "enemies" to present God's "Love" to. Therefore, Jesus was speaking to his disciples about the principles of God's "Love" and how they could measure their advancement in servitude to God, by individually living up to the lessons Jesus taught. Here, it is important to realize that one of Jesus' disciples was an "enemy," who was Judas Iscariot; and Jesus did not cast out Judas. Still, Jesus was not naively blind to that "enemy," who did nothing to overtly display where his heart was.

This focus on "Love" being maintained is then seen resurfacing in verses 32 and 33. According to the NIV translations, we are first told, "If you love those who love you, what credit is that to you? Even sinners love those who love them." In that verse, "love" is stated four times. However, this translation is a paraphrase and not what Jesus literally stated.

The Greek text says, "**Kai** *ei agapate tous agapōntas hymas , poia hymin charis estin ?*" The question posed in the second segment of words is based on fully understanding the statement prior. Where that statement begins with a hypothetical word ("if"), it is begun by a capitalized "*Kai*," which introduces a major statement to come. It should then be read as presenting "a BIG IF." That "IF" then supposes, "you love" (in the second-person plural in the present tense active voice) "those" (or "all") "loving" (in the present active participle accusative plural) "you" (in the second person plural pronoun of "*su*"). This means the important hypothetical is a statement of "If you are filled with God's 'Love'," which is a precondition set for all of Jesus' followers. It sets the bar as first being, "You are all truly Apostles with the Christ Mind."

The question that follows is then rhetorical, in the sense that given the disciples all being Saints (Apostles), "what credit is it to you?" That paraphrase misses how the question actually asks, "what to you gratitude exists ?" This question is then not about what "credit" one receives, because one has already been given the greatest gift possible (as the given in the hypothetical), which is the "Love" of God. The question from Jesus then posed the paraphrase, "What will you give back to God for His having blessed you?" As a rhetorical question, it answers itself as an indirect statement that means, "You do whatever God sends you to do with His "Love," because "gratitude" (from the Greek "*charis*") is the debt "you" owe God.

This then leads to Jesus say (NIV), "Even sinners love those who love them," which implies that "love" exists on a human level, capable of all "sinners." However, this "love" is not the same as God's "Love," which became the theme of this teaching in verse 27. This translation also misses the literal, which states: "*kai* all sinners (or those sinning, sinful, depraved, detestable) condition same cause." By realizing the importance marked by the Greek word "*kai*," and not translating that as a statement of equal "Love" (as "even"), this finishing statement in verse 32 says that demonstrating God's "Love" to "sinners" is the debt one owes to God, simply because all disciples, Saints, and Apostles were likewise "sinning, sinful, depraved and detestable" before they found Jesus and followed in his footsteps of "Love."

By understanding verse 32 in this way, it is then easy to grasp how verse 33 speaks of the "good" that comes from spreading God's "Love." There, Jesus said (NIV), "And if you do good to those who are good to you, what credit is that to you? Even sinners do that." Again, it should begin to be obvious how that translation is missing the marks of understanding, simply by seeing "And" and "Even" re-stated (incorrectly). The literal translation, which one can assume also includes another rhetorical question says, "*kai* for if you do that which is good to those doing good to you , what to you gratitude exists ?" This is not a statement warning against *quid pro quo* or doing a favor for a favor in return, but a statement leading to the rhetorical question that asks, "What good does preaching to the choir do?"

This makes the two statements with rhetorical questions found in verses 32 and 33 be a lesson to his disciples that being an Apostle of Saint is a blessing from God that is not meant for personal or private gain, but a gift from God for the purpose of that gift being shared. This lesson was an indirect slap at his "enemies," who did the opposite of what Jesus just stated. They do not have the "Love" of God with them, so they can only "love" those who give them positive reinforcement as return "love." They preach lessons memorized and standardized, which do not come with any instructions of clarifications needed by everyone seeking spiritual nourishment. They do not gratify God because they have no "Love" for or from Him.

Parables Explained: The Lesson to Love Your Enemies

This is a vital concept that needs to be pondered, because so much focus is placed on pacifying the "enemies" of a nation, as if God has given churches that use the name of Jesus Christ to offer blessings that will destroy that nation within its walls of defense. This is a Church that acts like a virus – a Trojan Horse – that promotes destruction in the name of Jesus. The real purpose Jesus was giving this lesson was to tell his disciples that their "enemies" were not Romans, or Syrians, or Persians, or Egyptians, or any other nation of the world; but instead, the "enemies" were those of the Temple in Jerusalem (and their supporters).

To drive home that realization, Jesus stated (importantly, via "*kai*"), "all sinners do the same." The Greek word "*hamartōloi*" is translated as "sinners" and it is found written four times in this verse about doing good and the next, which focus on lending. The Greek word "*hamartólos*" means "sinful" (Strong's definition), while intending to reflect "sinning, depraved, and detestable" also. (Strong's usage) According to HELPS Word-studies, the word "properly" states "loss from falling short of what God approves, i.e. what is "wide of the mark"; a blatant sinner." The use by Jesus should be seen as a statement about all human beings in the world (from "*hoi*"), from the same worldly state that all Christians arise; but this should also be read as a new focus being put on the "enemies" of those who possess God's "Love." More than identifying foreigners (or gentiles), Jesus is now making his disciples be compared to "sinners."

By realizing that the lessons of "Love" were being told to Jewish disciples that would become Christian Apostles, Jesus was telling them that they would become the ones having to deal directly with those who hated Jesus and his ministry. Rather than being watchful of those who clearly were hateful (much like how many Muslims openly hate Jews), the concept of "sinners" refers to those who know love from hate and good from bad (right from wrong). The blame of being sinful cannot be placed upon anyone who is ignorant of Jewish Law, as non-Jews are. This means "sinners" were other Jews, who Jesus and his disciples faced in synagogues and the Temple of Jerusalem.

This then transfers to our modern times as the individual's struggles with the churches of Christianity that do not (cannot) share the "Love" of God, simply because none have truly become filled with God's Holy Spirit. It is easily seen in the sports-like competitiveness that pits one denomination against another. Animosity exists commonly, such that Roman Catholics are seen as evil-doers by Protestants, and Roman Catholics will deny a non-Catholic the rite of Communion. It makes Christians hide their hatred, causing some to surface as false shepherds, with hidden agendas that seek to use inner sinfulness to further breakdown the Church of Christ. That is the light in which "enemies" and "Love" must be seen.

By having this concept firmly in hand, it becomes easy to understand why the trend in these similar verses then repeats in verse 34; but instead of "love" and "good" being given, Jesus changed to what appears to be loans of money. The NIV translation presents this as: "And if you lend to those from whom you expect repayment, what credit is that to you? Even sinners lend to sinners, expecting to be repaid in full." This opens the can of worms (nationally), where governments with laws based on Christian interpretations of the Laws of Moses (the Ten Commandments) then read this and enact laws that burden taxpayers with the responsibilities of giving financial support to immigrants and refugees. That is not what Jesus was teaching here.

Once again, it is easy to spot the repeated use of "And" and "Even," which is misleading and in need of translation adjustment. From the Greek text a literal translation can be found stating thus: "***kai*** if you lend (or borrow) alongside that you hope to receive , what to you gratitude exists ? ***kai*** sinners to sinners lend (or borrow) , so that they might receive condition equal ." In this breakdown into four segments of words, two of them importantly led by the word "*kai*," the listener-reader has to see the hypothetical focusing on the root Greek word "*danizó*," which means "to lend; to borrow." While the word implies the acts of loaning and borrowing, which may or may not be a statement of money exchanges, the word has to be seen as representing a business transaction. To lend or to borrow comes with the natural business expectation of payment for such loans, either interest paid back monetarily or more returned for access to what one needs immediately (eleven loaves of bread for the flour to make ten, for instance).

In this way, one has to see how this rhetorical question about what benefit can come from loaning a gift of God to other human being (the "sinners" of the world), when God is the source of that being lent? It becomes a four-segment series of statements that condense the parables of the minas (or talents) and the shrewd manager into a less figurative statement that God's business is for spiritual rewards. Regardless of how many worldly riches one seems to have been given by God's blessings, it amounts to the least of God's gifts: only one mina to bury (rather than invest) or all debts being renegotiated into profits. To turn the gift of the

Holy Spirit into a moneymaking business led Jesus to ask, "What gratitude [from God] comes if you expect to profit from God's blessings?"

This then becomes a huge statement that is not directed towards the mosques, synagogues, temples, or churches of the world, but to those who invest in religion by amassing material things: land, buildings, television stations, recording studios, limousines, vans, jet airplanes, etc. The borrowing and lending that is a natural way of the world is what "sinners" do. "Sinners to sinners borrow and loan." So, if Jim and Tammy Fae Bakker cry tears of woe about not having enough money to build Jesus World, or if another televangelist cries that he needs another fifty million dollars for a new personal jet plane to do God's work, or if a parish priest hires capital campaign donation professionals to get face-to-face with every parishioner with a dollar hidden away for a rainy day, they are all doing the business of "sinners." Equally, those who respond to those requests with dollars for lifetime passes to Jesus World, a chance to see a televangelist because he could fly into town on a private jet, or the luxury of sitting in a brand new pew in a beautiful new building, they have been repaid by worldly returns, which is what "sinners" can expect.

This must be seen as different than when Jesus said (NIV), "If someone takes your coat, do not withhold your shirt from them. Give to everyone who asks you, and if anyone takes what belongs to you, do not demand it back." In that scenario, where robes and tunics were the material statements of religious devotion, as priest of God (without diplomas), so anyone demanding those advertisements of religious values be removed (by force, if necessary), the context was clearly relative to "enemies" and showing them the "Love" of God by doing as they wish. The difference is in "giving," rather than "lending." God's "Love" is freely given to those who prove their "love" of God, but it is a gift that is given with the intent of it being further given, without expectations of worldly means. God's Word must be given to all who seek the truth, at no charge or with any expectations by the disciple through whom God's "Love" flows. Spiritual rewards will be paid in full after one's death in the flesh.

In this series of hypothetical situations of loving, doing good deeds and giving unto others freely, the "enemies" Jesus began to talk to his disciples about have transformed into "sinners." While "sinners" most readily translated in the minds of Jews as "Gentiles," the business of Jews was primarily with other Jews. The Jewish joke made by such Jewish comedians as Jerry Seinfeld is Jews always offer other Jews a special deal (wholesale profits), whereas the Gentiles will always be told to pay asking price (retail profits).

In Jesus' day, the Jews would never go to a Gentile to borrow money, and would barely be in a position to demand repayment from one if a loan was to be set up. This means the "enemies" one Jesus told his disciples to "love" are other Jews – the ones who demand they remove their robes of religious designation, expect the love of reverence as rulers, expect favors out of respect for their positions of power and authority, and expect payments on loans with interest, Thus, one "Loves" one's "enemies" simply by letting the scribes, Sadducees, and Pharisees do what they "love" to do and not get caught up in worry or fear, knowing God's "Love" is with his Apostles.

By seeing this, it is easy to see how Jesus transitioned to state, in verse 35 (NIV): "But love your enemies, do good to them, and lend to them without expecting to get anything back. Then your reward will be great, and you will be children of the Most High, because he is kind to the ungrateful and wicked." In that he returned to using the word "enemies" (Greek "*echthrous*"), with that word only said twice in this lesson. For as much as this lesson has been cut and pasted onto everyone in the entire world, as if Jesus had just told his disciples to follow the whims of everyone, out of a responsibility of "love," the reality is that the Jews that were Jesus and his disciples were restricted from going outside the Jewish world, even though that outside world would unavoidable come upon them. This summation then becomes a statement of usual activity with one's "enemies," who are "sinners," yet fellow Jews.

To see this supported in what Jesus said and what Luke wrote (inspired by the truth of the Holy Spirit), the syntax of standard human language has clouded what we commonly read, as that translated into English from the Greek. In verses 27 and 35 is written "*agapate tous echthrous hymōn*," with "*Agapate*" capitalized in verse 27 only. The English translates this as "love your enemies" (three words), when the Greek has four words that literally state: "love the enemies of you." In the paraphrase transition, the Greek pronoun "*hymōn*" is the genitive case form of "*su*," which "expresses possession or relation, equivalent to the English of." (Wiktionary.org) Rather than turn four Greek words into five English words, as "love the enemies of you," it becomes condensed as "love your neighbors." This clouds up who "you" is, which needs closer inspection.

There can only be "possession or relation" in the Jewish

Parables Explained: The Lesson to Love Your Enemies

disciples of Jesus, where "enemies" are concerned, when "enemies of you" are other Jews. One does not possess "enemies," but one can be related to them. Thus, both times Jesus told his Jewish disciple to "love the enemies of you," his intent was focused on those of the same religion that would make demands on those disciples and exert pressures on them to cease being like Jesus.

Jesus and his disciples (as Apostles) were seen as 'boat-rockers' and 'rebels' against the authority of the human beings that ruled Jerusalem and the Jews. They were then "enemies," as "sinners," because they attempted to force their will onto other Jews, as "enemies" to the power of God. That is how this lesson must be read, even though modern times have expanded the realm of "enemies" to just about everyone alive today. The reality is and will always be that the "enemies of you" are those who say they believe like you, making them relatives by their similar religious beliefs.

The reality of what Jesus summarized to his disciples is different that the paraphrase English of the NIV translation. First off, it is important to see that the capitalized Greek word "*Plēn*" begins these four segments, which has been translated as an important exception, as "But." The word is then read in the genitive as an adverb, meaning "More than, Above, Beyond, or Except" (Wiktionary.org), with Strong's adding "Yet" (definition) and "However" and "Nevertheless." In the capitalized form, the importance can apply to all, but makes good sense as "More than" or "Beyond," as an emphasis on the direction this teaching should go. With that read as the translation, the first segment is then an important focus on Jesus' first instruction, as "Beyond love the enemies of you."

All of the possibilities of translation for "*Plēn*" then become replacements for the capitalization of "*Agapate*," where it was read as God's "Love." The capitalized "*Plēn*" can now be read as along with "*agapate*" as relative to that most holy source, as being "More than love" [of human emotions], "Above love" [from God], "Beyond love" [capable of human sinners], "Except[ional] love," and "Nevertheless love" [that is on the lower plane of worldly existence]. That then becomes a contrast of "love enemies," as that combination acts as the pull and sway to move from "Above love" to become equals to "the enemies of you." It says for Apostles to rise "Above" one's "enemies" through the acceptance of God's "Love" as superior to human emotions and feelings. It, therefore, is not a command to capitulate to sin and "love enemies of you," where it is their sinfulness that all "sinners love" that must be avoided; and that can only come from help from "Above."

When that is understood, one can then see the second segment of words states, "***kai*** do good," where it is a one-word statement of importance, as "***kai*** *agathopoieite*." The word "*agathopoieite*" is in the second-person plural present active indicative and imperative, such that it acts as Jesus making an assertive command to act, as "do good!" After having stated, "Above love the enemies of you," this is not an 'also, oh by the way' "do good to your enemies." It is instead an important clarification that "Above love" does good things always. The root Greek word "*agathopoieó*" is stating, "I do that which is good" (Strong's usage), but that means "I do what is intrinsically good," or properly, "I do what is inherently good, i.e. is inspired and powered by God." (HELPS Word-studies)

Parables Explained: The Lesson to Love Your Enemies

The third segment of words in the summary is then equally an important one-word statement that is introduced by "*kai*," saying simply "lend (or borrow)." The Greek word written, "*danizete*," is likewise written in the second-person present active indicative and imperative, also acting as a command to act as a lender of God's Word. One is thus a borrower, as the Word of God is not one's to possess alone. The interest one owes for borrowing from God is paid by sharing freely what God lends to His Apostles. Therefore, unlike what Benjamin Franklin proposed – "Neither a borrower nor a lender be" – one must be in the business of listening to and speaking God's Word, where the profit is to be found in Heaven.

To cement that intent, following a comma make of separation the fourth segment of words states, "no one expecting in return," from the Greek words "*mēden apelpizontes*." Whereas the NIV translation leads one to thing Jesus said, "lend to them without expecting to get anything back," the reality is he commanded his disciples to love, do good, and give, all from the Father to the "sinners" among the Jews. In the natural sequence of things in those commands, there will be "no one" (from "*mēden*") who will be "expecting in return" either "love, goodness," or any return on investment from the Word shared freely. To join "lend" with this segment, as reading "*mēden*" as "nothing" or "not anything," the focus is then narrowed to "things," which neither "love" nor "goodness" are. As such, the Greek word "*apelpizontes*" is free to focus on expectations, which are freedom from despair and hope for rewards unseen. (Strong's usage)

This high expectation and freedom from the despair of sin then led Jesus to continue verse 35 with an address of this heavenly reward. The NIV translation says this begins by

Jesus stating, "Then your reward will be great." This is a fairly accurate translation, only lacking in the presentation of the first word being "*kai*," rather than a capitalized adverb of timing. What literally follows is the promise of what "will be" (from the Greek word "*estai*"), where the root focus is on the soul's future state of being. That future holds the "condition reward of you" (where the article "*ho*" is read again as "condition"), with "of you" (from "*hymōn*") being the religious collective that was the Jews. Instead of "great," the Greek word "*polys*" translates as "much or many," with the implication being a multitude or plentiful in quantity, as "great in amount." (Strong's usage and HELPS Word-studies)

When the NIV translation then says Jesus offered, "and you will be children of the Most High," the segment is again led by the important marker "*kai*." The Greek word "*Hypsistou*" is capitalized, so this personification becomes the name of God as the "Most High." Where the plural number that becomes a reflection of the "many" receiving the "reward" or "recompense" promised by God (the Greek word "*misthos*") is translated as "children." This translation supports the intent that "of you" is reference to the Jews, who identify themselves as the "children" of Israel. However, as it was Jesus telling this promise of God, the most accurate translation is as "sons of."

To better see this, the previous segment important foretold of the "reward" that "will be of you" ("*estai hymōn*"). I presented how this "reward" is better stated as "many," rather than "great." With "many" then understood as the number who will be "rewarded" by God ("Most High"), the plural number is fully stated next as "*esesthe huioi*," the "many" souls' future state of being will progress ("you will

Parables Explained: The Lesson to Love Your Enemies

be") from the Children of Israel (a worldly name or title) to "sons of" God ("Most High").

The word "*huioi*" is the plural form of "*huios*," which translates clearly as "a son," with this then generalized as a male "descendant." (Strong's definition and usage) HELPS Word-studies then adds depth to the understanding of this usage in a holy text, stating: "properly, a son (by birth or adoption); (figuratively) anyone sharing the same nature as their Father. For the believer, becoming a son of God begins with being reborn (adopted) by the heavenly Father – through Christ (the work of the eternal Son)." That source then adds how "sons" "equally refers to female believers." As Jesus is recognized by Christians to be the Son of God, Jesus was then promising the reward of his soul (the Christ Spirit) being joined with the souls of his Apostles (of both human genders), becoming a "multitude" of Jesuses reborn into the world. This is the truth of the word "Christianity."

The religion that has grown immensely since the ministry of Jesus of Nazareth ended with his death, resurrection and ascension has devolved to the state of merely being a club that believes in Jesus Christ. This belief seems to think Jesus' last name was "Christ," so all who believe Jesus was the Messiah are "Christians." The reality is, as seen here in the words Jesus spoke to his disciples (and in many other places in the Gospels and Epistles) says that his disciples would become Apostles that, like him, would be filled with the Holy Spirit of God and made most holy servants. The promise if they "will be sons of the Most High," where "sons" is not limited to male disciples.

A "son of God" is one who has been filled with God's Holy Spirit and made also the "Christ," given the knowledge of

God from which to proceed as an Apostle. Because Jesus was a human male, but more because God the **Father** represents the masculine principle of Spirituality (versus the feminine principle of the material universe), all who become the "Christ" will also bear this masculine identity, thus becoming "sons." Still, because Jesus is "THE Christ," as Jesus Christ, all who will become the "sons of the Most High" will be reborn as Jesus Christ, his Spirit united with the soul of another, becoming resurrected in the flesh of a follower. Thus, being truly **Christ**ian means being reborn in the name of Jesus Christ, which is a state far greater than a belief stemming from one's intelligence and education.

This understood, the NIV (and others) make an erroneous translation in the segment that reports Jesus saying, "because he is kind to the ungrateful and wicked." Some sources even capitalize "He" (from the lower-case Greek word "*autos*"), leading those who read this to conclude that God "is kind to the ungrateful and wicked." That becomes quite confusing, when the God of the Old Testament is routinely found leading Moses and others to punish "the ungrateful and wicked," raising the paradox seeming now created by Jesus' summary of God and one's "enemies."

The confusion disappears when the Greek text ("*hoti autos chrēstos estin epi tous acharistous* **kai** *ponērous*") is properly translated. Rather than fitting a mistaken conclusion based on an improper premise, the whole series of statements in this lesson are now found completely consistent. Immediately, based on my use of space and bold font to make the use of "*kai*" stand out, the last word places important focus on the word "wicked." Leading to that word is stated (in literal translation, maintaining the word order),

Parables Explained: The Lesson to Love Your Enemies

"that [being rewarded as the sons of God] self good [or serviceable] to be against all ungrateful [or ungracious]."

Clearly, the use of the Greek word "*hoti*," following a semi-colon mark that separate that word from "Most High," as a sign that two independent clauses are linked together as closely related thoughts, the translation as "that," as an introduction of a continuing discourse, means "that" directly refers to what had just been stated. The Greek word that has been translated as "kind" (NIV), "*chrēstos*," is a reference back to the earlier use of "*agathós*" (as "*agathopoieó*"), and the instruction to "do good." Here, the word "*chrēstos*" can also translate as "serviceable," which is a further statement that the "sons of Most High" are willing servants to the Lord. While that word can translate as "gentle, pleasant, and kind," it is better read as "useful." (Strong's definition, usage and HELPS Word-studies) Finally, the Greek word "*epi*," a directional preposition, has been translated simply as "to," when a better translation is "against." It is not confusing to grasp that God (through His servants) is "against" evil. Therefore a "self" (from the Greek "*autos*") that is "to be" (from the Greek "*estin*") will use God's "Love" and do "good" in response to all who have not experienced the "grace" of the "Most High."

When this clarity has come through, it is then easy to see that the "ungracious" (from the Greek "*acharistous*") are those so unblessed. The root word says they are "unpleasing," which would be their refusal to do God's Will or face God as His obedient subjects. (Strong's usage) Seeing how Apostles are said by Jesus to respond with good acts "against" their "enemies," the word is then most appropriate when seen to properly mean, "without God's grace (favor) which results in unthankfulness (literally, "ungraceful")." (HELPS Word-studies) They are then, importantly introduced by the word "*kai*," those who are "wicked" (from the Greek "*ponērous*"), which further defines them as "evil, bad, malicious, and slothful." (Strong's usage) HELPS Word-studies says the proper use of this one-word statement means, "pain-ridden, emphasizing the inevitable agonies (misery) that always go with evil." Therefore, it is only right that a true servant of God will fight "against" that ailment, rather than make one's sins worse.

The last verse in this lesson taught by Jesus to his disciples says (NIV), "Be merciful, just as your Father is merciful." In that translation, the first word is capitalized, which says "Be." The common capitalization of the first word os a sentence makes this statement of "Being" be overlooked and read simply as another instruction from Jesus, relative to how one should act. In reality, the Greek word "*Ginesthe*" is written, which needs a proper understanding.

That form of the Greek word "*ginomai*" is also in the second-person present active indicative and imperative, making it a command to act, as the realization of being that says, "I come into being, am born, become, come about, happen." (Strong's usage) HELPS Word-studies adds that the word means, "to emerge, become, transitioning from one point (realm, condition) to another," going further to state it "fundamentally means "become" (becoming, became) so it is not an exact equivalent to the ordinary equative verb "to be" (is, was, will be)." With this intent fully understood, the capitalization states the great importance of being "Reborn." That is then the reward that comes from having once been "wicked, sinful and evil," but died of that old "self" and sacrificed self-ego to "Become" an Apostle (Saint) of the Lord.

Parables Explained: The Lesson to Love Your Enemies

From seeing this meaning coming from the capitalized "*Ginesthe*," this state of new Being is then connected to the word "*oiktirmones*," which translates as "merciful," but also says "compassionate." When both words imply one acting in ways that offer mercy and compassion, the connection to the capitalized word of Rebirth has to be seen as it being God who has been "merciful" and "compassionate" to His servants. Therefore, Jesus was not instructing his disciple to show forgiveness to someone that could be harmed by one's power, but rather he was promising his devoted disciples that the Father would forgive their sins and have compassion for their self-sacrifices.

The final segment of words translated by the NIV is also missing the importance of an internal "*kai*." Their translation states, "just as your Father is merciful," which connects God to this state of mercy. However, the Greek text states, "*kathōs* **kai** *ho Patēr hymōn oiktirmōn estin*," where "*kathōs*" becomes a one-word statement that must be grasped.

The word translates as "just as," which is how it has been presented by the NIV. Still, it also states "according to" (Strong's definition) and is intended to imply "according to the manner in which and in the degree that." (Strong's usage) HELPS Word-studies then states of its proper intent: "in proportion, to the degree that" (J. Thayer); just as (in direct proportion), corresponding to fully (exactly)." This then says that the "Becoming merciful" is based on one having a duplication of God in the flesh, which makes one a copy of Jesus, "according to the manner in which" righteous human beings carry God's mercy to the world.

This is then confirmed in the following words that say, "***kai*** condition (from the Greek "*ho*") Father of you merciful is." The last word, "*estin*," has been used before, also stating "to be," which is relative to the "Rebirth" into a new state of being. As the "sons of Most High," here Jesus is restating that relationship through the resurrection of the Christ Spirit in true **Christ**ians, where the "condition" of Rebirth means the "Father of you" has mercifully bestowed His Holy Spirit. That new "you" then "is." Again, the mercy and forgiveness is totally the Father's to give, not human beings. Jesus, as a human being born with the Holy Spirit, as the promised Messiah, never acted as if he was in a position of power to forgive and show compassion to sinners. Instead, he always gave credit to the Father, which was the honor a Son must always observe.

With this in-depth analysis of what the actual Greek text from Luke's sixth chapter states, it should be clear that the paraphrase has become the fodder of political sermons that are regularly fed to the lost sheep. God did not send His Son into the world to save it globally from ruin. Sin is the ruin of the world and sin can only exist in that material state. God sent Jesus only to be the promised Messiah foretold for the Jews; Jesus said that. Simply based on that assertion ("I was sent only to the lost sheep of Israel," Matthew 15:24), Jesus would not be teaching his disciples about "enemies" beyond his scope of focus and one certainly has to see with clarity the people who constantly badgered Jesus were the one filled with hate for Jesus, who would plot his demise.

I must admit that prior to my doing this level of discern-

Parables Explained: The Lesson to Love Your Enemies

ment of the Greek text, I was convinced by logical deduction that one who is defined as "enemy" is so because of hatred of an individual or a group of like individuals. That hatred can never be absolved by attempts to convince one of a wrong mindset, demanding change. Enemies will always be enemies, because of innate reasons that are beyond the control of ideals and philosophies. Therefore, once one accepts that an enemy is like the opposite side of a coin, the only way to "love" an enemy is to allow that enemy to hate one from afar - give the enemy the space you would desire - avoiding any confrontation that wouldstir deep-rooted inner feelings.

By having one's eyes opened to this reality, knowing Jesus would not fill the minds of his closest followers with a philosophy of pacifisms that extended beyond the scope of their Jewish world, seeing Jesus teaching how Jews owe it to other Jews to help one another be found (not continue as lost sheep) is a sort of epiphany of dawning. The instruction found here in Luke is consistent with his other teachings, especially when Jesus was asked which of the Commandments was greatest. Jesus said:

> "Love the Lord your God with all your heart and with all your soul and with all your mind. This is the first and greatest commandment. And the second is like it: 'Love your neighbor as yourself. All the Law and the Prophets hang on these two commandments." (Matthew 22:37-40, NIV)

That instruction from Matthew will next be delved into, as it was what led Jesus to tell the parable of the good Samaritan, which will follow this lecture. What should be grasped from this statement by Jesus in Matthew above, relative to this breakdown of Luke 6:27-36, is Jesus told his disciples to "Love," which is a capitalized form of love that is greater than human love. That is his statement (in other words) to "Love the Lord your God with all your heart." With the first and greatest commandment reached, one can approach one's "enemies" with God's "Love."

When one realizes there is no mention of "enemies" in Jesus' response to the tricksters' question about the Law, it should be grasped that Jesus spoke of "neighbors" second. Jesus had said prior to this:

> "You have heard that it was said, 'Love your neighbor and hate your enemy.' But I tell you, love your enemies and pray for those who persecute you, that you may be children of your Father in heaven. He causes his sun to rise on the evil and the good, and sends rain on the righteous and the unrighteous." (Matthew 5:43-45)

There is mention in Exodus about "enemies" and those who "hate" one, but nothing is said that commands one to "hate your enemy." The truth of what Jesus said then is that the one's preaching "hate your enemies" were the Temple scribes, priests and the lawyers who owed their wealth to collective interpretations that projected themselves as the haters of Jerusalem. The Old Testament teachings (Commandments) said one should not let the fact that another Israelites is one's "enemy" and hates you keep one from helping an enemy. That is how one loves an enemy. It means an "enemy" is also a "neighbor." That is the lesson one has to gain from what Jesus said in Luke 6:27-36.

Parables Explained: The Lesson to Love Your Enemies

The Parable of the Good Samaritan

Luke 10:25-37

To fully understand how the enemies that Jesus spoke of in Luke's sixth chapter were fellow Jews, the parable of the Good Samaritan becomes proof. Luke has the least consistent chronologically of the four Gospels, told almost as if an elderly Saint Mary told her biographer (also a saint) of her son's ministry, with the occasional aside. That explains how some events, told by other saints as happening before or after, appear in an odd position of timing. Still, the chronology of Jesus' life up to the telling of this parable clearly lists some prior events and lessons that are important to review first, in order to help guide one in this interpretation of Luke's words. The history leading up to Luke 10:25 should be reviewed first.

In Luke's ninth chapter, verses 51 to 56, Jesus sent messengers out before him in his travels. Jesus had been well north of Galilee, in the region of Perea north of Caesarea Philippi. It was on Mount Hermon (the high mountain that dwarfs Mount Tabor) that Jesus had been transfigured, and he knew he was returning to Jerusalem for another confrontation with the Temple's elite. As the trek would be southward, messengers had been sent "into a Samaritan village to get things ready for" Jesus' arrival. (Luke 9:52, NIV)

Parables Explained: The Parable of the Good Samaritan

We then find: "The people there [Samaritans] did not welcome [Jesus], because [Jesus] was heading for Jerusalem." (Luke 9:53, NIV) The disciples James and John [of Zebedee] saw this and asked Jesus, "Lord, do you want us to call fire down from heaven to destroy them?" (Luke 9:54, NIV) However, we read: "Jesus turned and rebuked them," taking "his disciples … to another village." (Luke 9:55-56)

That event says, indirectly, that the Samaritans were the enemies of the Jews. Both groups had learned to hate one another, in particular because the Jews had outcast the Samaritans for having lost their land (Israel) and blended with their captors, rather than remaining pure. The Samaritans saw that as hypocritical, since the Jews had likewise been taken into Babylon, where they were forced to assimilate with foreign (gentile) ways. Both groups of people were descended from the children of Israel (Abraham, Isaac and Jacob), led by Moses, Aaron and Joshua to the Promised Land, which their forefathers had then split and lost. They were enemies, but they worshipped the same YHWH.

Samaria was where the Israelites recognized holy days of the Covenant in Bethel, only twelve miles north of Jerusalem. The first king of the Northern Kingdom (Jeroboam) made an altar there, where Jacob dreamed of a ladder to heaven. For Jewish disciples (messengers) to be sent to enter a Samaritan village and ask for supplies for Jesus, who was just going to be passing through, the anger of enemies raised the Samaritan villagers to "not welcome Jesus." When James and John suggested an equal response of anger (based on Elijah having done the same thing against the prophets of Baal), the rebuke of Jesus was due to the brothers having not grasped his teaching prior. When Jesus instead took his travel group "to another village," it was done out of love for enemies (of the same religious faith). It is vital to understand this animosity between Jews and Samaritans, and why it existed.

In this rebuke by Jesus, where that word is translated from the Greek root "*epitimaó*," basically meaning he made a "warning to prevent something from going wrong" (HELPS Word-studies), it must be noticed that Jesus did not let a mistake go uncorrected. As the rabbi (teacher) of the disciples, whose voice was that of the Father, it is vital to realize that should a child attempt to escape punishment by saying, "I hate you daddy! However, don't forget that Jesus said love your haters!" it would mean a minimum of a verbal rebuke. James and John of Zebedee were punished by a warning, for not loving their enemies. Jesus used punishment to correct their absence of God's "Love." Therefore, one should not conclude that the wrongs of one's enemies should be condoned and forgiven when they are wrongs based on hatred. The response to a loved one is set him or her straight, but the response to an enemy is to go in another direction, avoinding making matters worse.

Second, Luke 10 begins with the story of Jesus sending out seventy-two disciples in ministry. In verse three Jesus said to those disciples, "Go! I am sending you out like lambs among wolves." (Luke 10:3, NIV) The use of "lambs" and "wolves" has to be seen as the opposites of prey and predator, where both live on the same land, wary of the potential for violent confrontation. The symbolism that reflects the truth of that statement needs to be realized.

The Greek word "*arnas*," which translates as "lambs," should be read as children of Israel. When Jesus was in the north, around Sidon and Tyre, he had said, "I was sent only

Parables Explained: The Parable of the Good Samaritan

to the lost sheep of Israel." Jesus said that to a Canaanite woman who pleaded to him for her daughter's health. (Matthew 15:22-24) Jesus said he was the Good Shepherd, which means his disciples were his lambs and the Jews of Judea and Galilee (and elsewhere) were the lost sheep. He would send out the seventy-two disciples as lambs, carrying with them nothing to have the lost sheep think they were predators in disguise, allowing them to be welcomed by those lost.

The Greek word "*lykōn*" translates as "wolves," but more than an expectation of dangerous wild animals attacking unarmed disciples, the use is metaphor for "cruel, greedy, rapacious, destructive men." (HELPS Word-studies) That usage intended, the expectation would be for the Jewish disciples to go out into places where Jewish settlements were. That made the "wolves" be representative of the enemies of other Jews bearing news – "The kingdom of God has come near."

This makes the root word from which "*lykōn*" comes, "*leukos*," be an identification of what the "wolves" would look like. The word "*leukos*" means "bright, white, brilliant," as a descriptive term for the white hair found on "wolves." This makes "white haired wolves" be a good description of those who were considered elders, many of whom maintained power by feeding the Temple rulers with warnings of dissident actions about.

This assessment can then be found accurate, after the seventy-two had returned with the news of having great powers over demons, leading Jesus to call them together privately. In the privacy of the group, Jesus prayed a prayer of thanks to God for this success. In that prayer he said, "I praise you, Father, Lord of heaven and earth, because you have hidden these things from the wise and learned, and revealed them to little children." (Luke 10:21, NIV) In that statement by Jesus, the use of "little children" (from the Greek "*nēpiois*") should again be seen as metaphor, which relates to the "lambs" sent out among "wolves." This means "the wise" (from the Greek "*sophōn*") is descriptive of the "wolves," which needs closer inspection.

Thayer's Greek Lexicon states a common purpose for the use of "*sophos*" (their 'B' definition) was to identify as "wise" those who are "skilled in letters, cultivated, and learned." As such, during the times of Jesus, especially in the contexts of the Holy Bible's New Testament, the "wise" were "of the Jewish theologians." This then relates "white haired wolves" to those who were learned in the writings of the Torah. However, knowledge of scrolls was not evidence of closeness to God, such that only that relationship would allow one to understand the writings on the scrolls; and the "wise" had that knowledge "hidden" from them, whereas the "little children" of Jesus had meaning revealed to them, in service to the Father.

Jesus then ended his private conversation-prayer by telling his disciples, "For I tell you that many prophets and kings wanted to see what you see but did not see it, and to hear what you hear but did not hear it." (Luke 10:24, NIV) This warning should be seen as an explanation that lets his followers know that the "wise" are not their friends. Because of their state of immaturity – being "little children" in the realm of memorization and study of written scrolls and the scholarly discussions about what the meaning is – makes their unexplained abilities be greatly at odds with the scribes and priests of the Temple and their lawyer friends,

Parables Explained: The Parable of the Good Samaritan

the Sadducees and Pharisees. Just as they attacked Jesus and tried to trick him into heretical answers, as "white haired wolves" that were his enemies, Jesus warned his followers to expect the same rejection. Having the powers of God at one's disposal will not make everyone who professes belief in Yahweh to be friendly, especially if loss of riches and influence are at stake.

It is then with all of this supporting information that one should begin to address the verses in Luke's tenth chapter, leading to Jesus telling the Parable of the Good Samaritan. In that regard, verse 25 begins by stating, "On one occasion an expert in the law stood up to test Jesus" (Luke 10:25a, NIV), where one is now aware that "an expert of the law" is one of those "wolves" Jesus' "lambs" had been sent out amongst. It is also one of the "wise" who is a "learned theologian" of Judaism. It is also an enemy that feels it is his place "to test Jesus," where the Greek word "*ekpeirazōn*" ("testing") implies "going to improper measures which exceed appropriate boundaries and pushing the one tested beyond reasonable (proper) limits." (HELPS Word-studies)

The simplified translation of the New International Version (NIV) misses some important nuisances that the Greek text offers. Rather than stating, "On one occasion," verse 25 is more closely related to verse 24, where Jesus privately told his disciple how there were those who wanted to see and hear like them but could not. In verse 25 a capitalized "*Kai*" begins it, making one be aware that great importance is to follow. The one word that follows "*Kai*" is "*idou*," which becomes an important one-word statement (due to a comma following it) that says, "See! Lo! Behold! Look!" with capitalization and exclamation point marks implied. After Jesus had just said there are those who want "to see" (from the Greek "*iden*"), a divinely inspired Luke then exclaimed, "Behold! Exactly what Jesus was talking about!"

Seeing this important announcement that is missed in the NIV Luke then wrote more than simply stating, "an expert in the law stood up." His Greek text literally states in English, "a lawyer certain stood up" (from the Greek "*nomikos tis anestē*"). Here, the word "*nomikos*" is a word that conveys "one who is learned in the Law," unlike how the word "lawyer" today does not yield that inference. The NIV adds "expert" to make this assumption better understood. However, that translation into English overlooks the word "*tis*," seeing that as a statement of "one."

The reality of "*tis*" is it requires a translation as "certain." That says how amid Jesus' disciples was one who practices as a "lawyer." As a disciple of Jesus' the "lawyer" was known by everyone else as that. However, the most often intent of "certain" is to identify a Jew, with Thayer's Greek Lexicon stating it means "certain one, used of persons and things concerning which the writer either cannot or will not speak more particularly."

In this identification of a "lawyer" that was known by Jesus and his disciples, thought to be one of them as followers and believers in Jesus, separate from those who were Jewish but disbelievers, it is important to see how Luke is about to recount the story often called "Jesus and the young, rich man," told in Luke's eighteenth chapter (Luke 18:18-29) and also in the Gospels of Matthew (Matthew 19:16-22) and Mark (Mark 10:17-27). This is then a separate story that differs from Luke's second version, where the person is identified as "a ruler," implying "an official member of the assembly of elders" [the Sanhedrin]. Mat-

Parables Explained: The Parable of the Good Samaritan

thew and Mark do not identify the man by his wealth or influence, but tell of the "young man" walking away from Jesus because he had many possessions. Here, there is no mention of that walking away, nor the instructions given by Jesus that would guarantee admission into God's eternal kingdom.

While the "lawyer" is not directly identified by any of the Apostles, other than here in Luke's tenth chapter, "a lawyer" among Jesus' disciples would be named in the Gospels somewhere. That scholarly position would make the "lawyer" a Pharisee, who tended to be attracted to Jesus (not usually for good reasons) but largely unnamed. Two are named that make this "lawyer" become more "certain" than simply being a Jewish scholar of Law. The two named that can be identified as possible are Joseph of Arimathea and Nicodemus. Because Mark named Joseph and said he was "a respected member of the council, who was also himself waiting expectantly for the kingdom of God," and Luke added Joseph "had not agreed to [the Sanhedrin's] plan and action," and John wrote that he "was a disciple of Jesus, though a secret one because of his fear of the Jews," this confirms that Joseph was most likely the one who is named by Luke here as "a certain lawyer."

I believe that Nicodemus plays a role in this circumstance later. Because Joseph and Nicodemus were together in the preparation of Jesus' body for burial, they most likely were a pair of disciples that, due to their positions as high-ranking Pharisees, had to maintain a low profile as Jesus followers. Without any direct proof as to a specific identity, one should gather from this story being told by Luke, the physician of Mother Mary (also an Apostle later), that this "lawyer" had not fully committed his true allegiance to that group, although Jesus was a mesmerizing presence to be around. The identification as "a certain lawyer" would not only be a way to maintain the secrecy of someone like Joseph and Nicodemus as disciples of Jesus, but this report acts to expose a known Pharisee was among this group of disciples. It says that doubt still existed in those who had more worldly possessions at risk, with that doubt remaining hidden within a pair like Joseph and Nicodemus.

This story is then a follow-up example of how that which had been hidden will be exposed by God, so the "little children" of Jesus will see how easy it is for a wolf to hide amongst the lambs. We know that Judas Iscariot was a secret enemy who would be known in the hindsight of the disciples becoming Apostles. Still, it is doubtful that Joseph could maintain his secrecy as a Jesus follower if he had been paired with anyone of lesser means, as that pairing would stand out quickly. One "lawyer" would then be paired with a second, who did not "stand up" as Jesus was teaching them. As such, it is worthwhile to intuit that minimally one of the seventy-two was a spy for the Temple elite, rather than being a devout follower of Jesus (or God).

When we read that the lawyer "stood up" (from the Greek "*anestē*") the meaning has to be seen as he had been in a sitting (or reclining) position. Because we have studied the text of Luke 10 prior to this first verse of this section, we can intuit that when Jesus turned to his disciples to speak in "private" (from the Greek "*idian*") to the group of seventy-two, who then took seats surrounding him. The word "*idios*" can equally mean in a "personal" address (Strong's usage), with the word also being used to denote "one's own family, home, property." (HELPS Word-studies)

Parables Explained: The Parable of the Good Samaritan

Because this verse is divided at this point, with a comma mark following "stood up," it makes a point of emphasizing this act. It means Jesus was not speaking to the seventy-two in a public area, as he probably took his disciples into a place secured in Jerusalem (Essene Quarter) or in Bethany. This concept is supported by Luke following this lesson and parable of the Good Samaritan with Jesus and his disciples going to the home of Martha and Mary.

The word "*anestē*" can mean to rise up from death, but that is not supported in the surrounding context. It therefore means rising from a low position, often from a bed after sleep. Thayer's Greek Lexicon says about the root verb, "*anistémi*," its use means it speaks "of those about to enter into conversation or dispute with anyone." In that use, that source lists Luke 10:25 as an example. While a confrontation can simply be a question posed to "stand forth" to Jesus, it gives the impression of a student rising before his teacher to challenge him. The comma's sign to pause at that word adds to this inference.

Following the comma mark is the Greek word "*ekpeirazōn*," which is the active present participle verb that translates as "testing" or "putting to the test." The third-person masculine pronoun "*auton*" is then free to mean both "him" the one standing up and "him" Jesus. The strongest intent of the pronoun is a reference to the "certain lawyer," simply because the comma mark leads to a one-word statement that is the Greek word "*legōn*," which is again a verb stated in the present active participle – "saying" or "speaking." This says the "certain lawyer" was remembering how Jesus had just told the group that important people ("prophets *kai* kings") wanted to see what the seventy-two had seen and hear what the seventy-two had heard, all relative to the "wise" that did not know more than "little children." After Jesus had given thanks to God for the Holy Spirit having been with seventy-two novices and remarking privately about what a blessing they had experienced, a "certain lawyer stood up" amid the group and asked Jesus a question.

Before going into the address made prior to the question, it is worthwhile to ponder on how a disciple that had been sent out to minister to the lost sheep of Israel (scattered Jews in Galilee and Judea) and experienced the power to make demons fear their presence, while the Holy Spirit worked through their minds and mouths preaching the meaning behind "the kingdom of God has come near," would not know the answer to the question he was about to pose. For a "certain lawyer" to feel equal to Jesus that he should either stand up or raise a question says volumes about his being a spy in the midst of the seventy-two.

Keeping in mind how Judas Iscariot was a traitor waiting for a chance to exploit Jesus, while stealing from the contributions that were made to support the movements of Jesus and his disciples, his role as treasurer would have certainly put him in touch with "lawyers" among the disciples, because they would have funding to share. Since Judas Iscariot would play the role of 'devil's advocate' within the closest disciples of Jesus, he most likely would spread doubt among the peripheral disciples and family followers. Simply by a "certain lawyer" rising up to ask the question about how he will know he will be assured of heaven, says the snake of doubt had whispered into his ear. With doubt keeping someone like Joseph from fully committing to Jesus, the question then becomes a statement that the "lawyer" could not have experienced the bliss of the Holy Spirit within him, like that reported to Jesus by the others. If he indeed went out in ministry, he must have failed to have demons flee his presence; but it is more likely that he was paired with another like him (like the "lawyer" Nicodemus) and the two of them did nothing ministerial; instead they wrote letters that were sent to the Temple, updating them as to Jesus' whereabouts. This is how one can 'read between the lines' of Scripture, by closely observing the details of what is written, rather than thinking "hurry up and get to the moral of the story."

From this deeper reflection on the motivation of the "certain lawyer," it is possible to see how another one-word statement follows "saying" or "speaking." The Greek word that follows, set apart by bookend comma marks, is "*Didaskale*," which translates as "Teacher." The definition of this word is "an instructor" (Strong's definition), but the intent (especially with capitalization) is as "Master." HELPS Word-studies adds the meaning to be "a teacher, an instructor acknowledged for their mastery in their field of learning; in Scripture, a Bible teacher, competent in theology." It is in Scripture where this is found written, so further analysis is warranted in this case.

Simply by Luke having stated that a "certain lawyer stood up" to ask a question of Jesus, he was knowledgeable of the Laws of Moses, or the Torah. That was the meaning of his being recognized as "a lawyer" (from the Greek word "*nomikos*"). It is, therefore, a statement of this man's knowledge of the Law that he has risen from a student's position, as if "saying", "Hold on here a minute. I am a qualified "Teacher" of the Law, as "a lawyer." This means the question about to be posed is as if the "lawyer" knew the answer beforehand and was presenting Jesus with a "test" of his knowledge. The question is then "testing," as the "lawyer" (from all his expertise of studying the Law) does not expect the question can be answered, making it a trick question. The purpose of a trick question at this point would be to make Jesus appear to seventy disciples (minus the "lawyer" and Judas) as not quite so learned as they thought.

The other element that comes forward from the capitalization of a one-word statement that says "Teacher" or "Master" is it presumes (in a setting where all persons are Jewish) to be a statement of "Rabbi." In John's Gospel (John 20:16) and in Mark's Gospel (Mark 10:51) one finds the word "*rabbouni*" written (neither time capitalized, understood as Aramaic), but the concept of Jewish "teachers" was just getting off the ground in the first century (during the days of Jesus). This means all Jewish children had "rabbis," in the sense that the Law needed to be taught from early childhood to adulthood, much like today's system of public education. As a "teacher," there was no pronouncement of superiority (just as American teachers today lag far behind the salaries paid in other careers requiring diplomas), as all Jewish adults knew the Laws that had been taught, with none of those laws having changed.

It was the "lawyers" that supported the Temple that debated questions of "Law," with none of them seen as special because of intellectual arguments presented (wealth was the only measuring stick they honored). The Pharisees, Sadducees and Essenes were all different camps of philosophical discernments of the Law that set them apart. Thus, the capitalization here by Luke must be seen as the divinity of Jesus as a "Master," while also being a statement that "a certain lawyer" also saw himself as divine, based on his

Parables Explained: The Parable of the Good Samaritan

knowledge, wealth, and influence brought about by his personal allegiance to a certain sect of Jewish philosophers.

When the NIV then states the question posed as, "what must I do to inherit eternal life?" an important element is ignored. Rather than asking "what must I do," the Greek words written by Luke state (separated by comma marks), "what having done" (from the Greek words "ti poiēsas"). Because "poiēsas" is stated in the past tense participle (aorist verb) it is not projecting what needs to be done in the future, but a statement of what has already been done. As the "lawyer" is in a group of seventy-two men that had been sent out with the power of the Holy Spirit and successfully returned to Jesus, the question predisposes that fact as a given. This also then leans back to the capitalized "Teacher" statement, where having been sent out in ministry seems to qualify all of the seventy-two as equals, with all being "Teachers."

The question is now changed to "will I inherit eternal life?" (from the Greek words *"zōēn aiōnion klēronomēsō,"* or literally "life eternal will I inherit"). The Greek word *"zōēn"* focuses on the spiritual nature of future "life" (Strong's usage), as "sustained by God's self-existent life." (HELPS Word-studies) By clarifying that with "eternal" (from the Greek "aiōnion"), the trick of the "testing" is to see if Jesus can answer this age-old uncertainty of the afterlife.

The Pharisees believed in Sheol, whereas the Sadducees believed there was no afterlife. According to Josephus, the Essenes believed the soul was both eternal and preexistent, meaning they believed in reincarnation. As Jesus was most likely an Essene, the trick would be to have Jesus expose his philosophical beliefs, and explain how being like Jesus in ministry would deem one worthy of Heaven, not having to come back and start all over again in human flesh. Because reincarnation was deemed by the Essenes to be an admission of failure, as far as living life righteously, the "certain lawyer" asked, in essence, "Does this success we all just had justify us as being confident we will go to Heaven?"

By Luke having the "lawyer" stating the Greek word "*klēronomēsō*," which translates as "will I inherit," the implication is an expectation of gain by birthright. The Greek root word implies "a specific allotment of inheritance, apportioned by casting lots" (HELPS Word-studies), where sons are given a tiered amount of paternal possessions, based on birth order, rather than all sons receiving the same. Still, the usual expectation of inheritance is to wait until the father passes away and do only what is required by the father while he is alive, so the father will not cut one out of the will. This view of human inheritance was then set into the question that was relative to God the Father and a promise to gain eternal life through commitment to the Covenant made with the Children of Israel. As such, the question excluded gentiles from this expectation, while posed as an indirect statement of expectations from Yahweh, based on the luxury promise the Jews inherited, as descendants.

Such a question should be seen as a trap for Jesus to fall into, such that the "lawyer" expected him to set all his disciples free from following him (no longer needing Jesus to get to Heaven) or dash all their hopes for their sacrifices already made from having followed him (if having great spiritual powers over others was not a sign of great promises already rewarded by Yahweh). Again, one should see

Parables Explained: The Parable of the Good Samaritan

this question posed as without any expectation of an answer that would take the "lawyer's" breath away. He probably was a Pharisee, because a fellow Essene would not pose such a question to Jesus, knowing that entering God's eternal kingdom is a matter totally in God's hand, with life in the flesh always to demand more obedience through servitude and devotion. Therefore, any answer given by Jesus was expected to fail miserably.

With that question posed, Jesus answered with the question: "What is written in the Law?" Jesus, as the "Teacher" knew his disciple was "a lawyer," so the question posed for the benefit of the whole group was turned back onto the "lawyer," because he thought of himself as a "Teacher" of the Law. This means Jesus was "testing" his student by that question. Still, Jesus followed that global 'legal' question with a clarification question asking, "How do you read it?"

The Greek words written by Luke in this clarifying question are "*pōs anaginōskeis?*" which literally can translate to ask, "how you read?" On a deeper level of discernment, the word "*pōs*" asks "by what means" or "in what manner" (Strong's usage), where "how" becomes a question aimed less at the mechanics of reading and more about what techniques of reading for comprehension one employs. From that grasp of the intent of the clarifying question, the word "*anaginōskeis*" can be read as meaning "you know again, you know certainly, you recognize, or you discern." (Strong's usage)

When this is understood, both questions can be seen as the "Teacher" giving the student the answers sought, by phrasing the answers as questions. This says the answer to inheriting eternal life is found in "what is written in the

Law." The truth of that is then based on "how you read [it]." This is not coincidence and should be seen as the way God speaks in Scripture, where what can be discerned one day will often (if not always) offer something new, something missed before, at others times of deep reflection on the Word.

The questions by Jesus then elicited the following response by the "lawyer," seemingly proud that he quickly was able to answer Jesus. He said (according to the NIV English translation): "Love the Lord your God with all your heart and with all your soul and with all your strength and with all your mind; and, Love your neighbor as yourself." This is important to dig deeper into.

First of all, the answer given by the "lawyer" to Jesus is exactly the same answer given by Jesus to a Pharisee, after he overheard Jesus give a good answer that silenced the Sadducees. The chronology of Matthew and Mark, who recorded that question and answer event had the timing of happening after Jesus had entered Jerusalem triumphantly, prior to his last Passover there. The Greek text from those two Gospels state Jesus said:

> "*Agapēseis kyrion ton Theon sou en holē tē kardia sou , kai en holē tē psyche sou , kai en holē tē dianoia sou . hautē estin hē megalē kai prōtē entolē . duetera de homoia autē : Agapēseis ton plēsion sou hōs seauton .*" (Matthew 22:37-39)

> "***kai*** *agapēseis Kyrion ton Theon sou ex holēs tēs kardias sou ,* ***kai*** *ex holēs tēs psyches sou ,* ***kai*** *ex holēs tēs dianoias sou ,* ***kai*** *ex holēs tēs ischyos sou . duetera hautē : Agapēseis ton plēsion*

Parables Explained: The Parable of the Good Samaritan

sou hōs seauton ." (Mark 12:30-31)

The same basic words are written in the same order, with Matthew writing in the singular and Mark in the plural. Mark capitalized "*Kyrion*" (as did Luke), but Matthew used the lower case "*k*." Marks added, "and with all your strength," which Matthew omitted. Matthew added, "The second also is like it," while Mark wrote, "Second this."

Here, in Luke's tenth chapter, Jesus was still nine chapters away from triumphantly entering Jerusalem for his last Passover. In an impromptu questioning by a disciple that was "a certain lawyer," Jesus asked the student about the Law and what he got from it, relative to gaining "eternal life" in Heaven. That "lawyer" gave the answer that Jesus would give in the future, saying in the Greek of Luke:

> "*Agapēseis Kyrion ton Theon sou ex holēs tēs kardias sou* , **kai** *en holē tē psychē sou* , **kai** *en holē tē ischui sou* . **kai** *en holē tē dianoia sou* **kai** *Ton plēsion sou hōs seauton* ." (Luke 10:27)

This answer given to Jesus is a blend of what Jesus would say, as per Matthew and Mark (and Luke again), with the plural number being used at first (Mark), before switching to the singular (Matthew). The "lawyer" added what Matthew had omitted but Mark remembered, but he switch the "strength" and "mind" parts. Rather than repeat "Love" ("*Agapēseis*") as the precursor to the "second" most important Commandment, Luke had him lead with "*kai*," then capitalize "*Ton*." That connects "Love" to the "second," without making it another Commandment from the Law, while making the weal personal pronoun "Him" (from "*Ton*") represent the singular and the plural of those who study the Law.

Again, this is not coincidence that makes a disciple ("lawyer" nonetheless) say the exact same thing as Jesus would answer later to a Pharisee. It is an example of the power Jesus had as the Son of God, thus the true "Teacher." It was Jesus that was leading the one who "stood up" to say what God wanted His Sons to say, relative to what the Laws were meant to be. It is comparable to Peter, when asked by Jesus (as one of the twelve) listening to the question, "Who do you say I am?" Peter blurted out because Jesus wanted the answer to that question to come through the lips of another, via the Holy Spirit. Peter said, "You are the Messiah, the Son of the living God," when he was too afraid to say what he had told others who Jesus was. Likewise, the "lawyer," if not controlled by the Mind of Christ to say what he said, probably would have stammered and said, "Well, gee. I don't know. That's why I was asking you."

By seeing that the "certain lawyer" was "tested" by Jesus, such that instead of the "lawyer" being led into a trap he (like the example of Peter) was led to speak the truth of the Holy Spirit. He gave the true answer to his own question, exactly as Jesus stated (posing as a question), "You get out of the Law what you let the Holy Spirit lead you to realize" (or "How read you"). This then allowed the "Teacher" to use an attempt to upstage him to go into praising the disciple not blocking the Holy Spirit from flowing through him.

Jesus said (according to the NIV), "You have answered correctly. Do this and you will live." This paraphrase misses some more important elements that need to be pointed out.

Parables Explained: The Parable of the Good Samaritan

Jesus said (and Luke wrote) the Greek word "*Orthōs*" first, which is capitalized, showing the importance of the "Correctness" of his answer. The word does bear that usage, but is better seen as powerful when translated as "Rightly." (Strong's definition and usage) It is only read as "correctly" when seen figuratively in translation. (Strong's Exhaustive Concordance) The capitalization as "Rightly" is then a statement of the truth having been stated, with a strong lean towards moral correctness, more than memorized teachings.

The answer given by the "lawyer" was not an educated statement, such that all "lawyers" would give the response he had just given. No "lawyer" would say his study of the Law had led him to conclude that reading it clearly says to "Love God." No one would ordinarily spew a series of statements about "Love of God" should always represent a total commitment from one's heart, soul, strength, mind, **and** one's ability to be "Him" that treats his neighbor as himself. Those answers are combined from Deuteronomy 6:5 and Leviticus 19:18, where that separation in holy texts says no student of the Torah would have deduced only those two laws as the keys to the answer to the question "Will I inherit eternal life?" Just as Peter came up with an answer he would have never thought of, the Holy Spirit rushed into their mouths and let the truth come forth. That made their answers "Rightly answered."

The simplicity of Jesus seeming to say "Do this and you will live" misses the separation created by a comma mark, with the comma followed by the marker word "*kai*." When one realizes that Jesus first said "this do" (from the Greek words "*touto poiei*"), the answer stated by the "certain lawyer" by the Holy Spirit was "telling" all the disciples listening, "construct a path of righteousness that meets the demands of God's Commandments just stated." It is then the "acts" of Apostlehood that transform one from the assured 'death-reincarnation-death-reincarnation' cycle that is mistakenly called "life." Thus, one must act according to the Law first; then "you will live."

This second statement is led by the importance of the word "*kai*," with a powerful one-word statement introduced that says "you will live" (from the Greek word "*zēsē*"). The word "*zēsē*" is the future active indicative of "*zaó*," meaning the acts of righteousness, as taught by the Law, will definitely bring true life in the future. This not only means one "will live" in Heaven, but one will cease being a walking zombie that has nowhere to go with an eternal soul, once its host body of flesh dies (an inevitability). To cease being a warm body of death walking and talking, pretending that is life, one has to have an epiphany of realization that Holy Scripture is written by prophets and requires prophets to understand what is written. That epiphany comes from episodes like the "certain lawyer" just had, so one begins to see the brain is only in the way, blocking one's soul from the reward of eternal life away from the binds of flesh. This means dying of self-ego, so the death of material desires within a human body allows the soul to be filled with God's Holy Spirit and experience true life, which means walking in righteousness until physical death frees that soul from a body of limitation.

After Jesus had told the "certain lawyer" that he had given the right answer and all he had to do from then on was live up to his own statement, based on the Law, we then read the NIV English translation having the "lawyer" realize that somehow Jesus had completely turned the table on him.

Parables Explained: The Parable of the Good Samaritan

The reading then states, "But he wanted to justify himself." The Greek of this statement is "*Ho de thelōn dikaiōsai heauton,*" where the capitalized 'article' "*Ho*" is seen as superfluous and completely ignored. Instead the capitalization is transferred to "*de*" and translated as a simple conjunction of exception – "But." This is a matter that needs correction.

The Greek word "*ho*" is said by the Bill Mounce website's Greek Dictionary to be: "(often not translated) the, this, that, who." The NAS Exhaustive Concordance, as the NASB Translation list for other possible translations of "*ho, hé, to*" includes "all (5), circumstances (3), companions (8), condition (1), some (12), others (5), those (406), those who (17), what (48), and who (52)" [among others]. It is through these alternative ways of reading a capitalized "*Ho*" that the Greek statement written by Luke should be read, as nothing in holy Scripture is superfluous.

The Greek word "*de*" has been capitalized in translation as "But," read as another word of seeming little significance. That word is a conjunction that typically translates as "but, and, now" (Strong's definition), but it too should be more directed in translation by the usage applied to "*Ho.*"

Seeing that need, the literal translation into English can now be read as "Condition now intending to defend the cause of himself." This takes the translation of the Greek word "*dikaiōsai,*" which has been translated in the NIV as "to justify," and gives that word more clarification as "to defend the cause." The verb is written in the aorist (past) tense active infinitive mood, such that the "lawyer," upon hearing himself answer what his brain was incapable of calculating, was "desiring (intending) to be righteous (to justify) himself," then ("now") at that point in time, because of the importance of the "Rightly" answer that came through "Him" (from "*Ton*"), as a "Condition" (from "*Ho*") to "inherit eternal life." This says the "lawyer" immediately felt the "desire" or "want" (from the Greek "*thelōn*") to go forward as a changed man, "to put himself into a right relationship with God" (Parsing & Meaning for "δικαιῶσαι" ["*dikaiōsai*"] stated by the website misslebrook.org.uk)

From seeing the epiphany that then came to this "certain lawyer" it is clear to see how he then asked Jesus, importantly because the question is led by a capitalized "*Kai*," "who is my neighbor?" This is the key reason that Jesus would then tell the parable of the Good Samaritan as this "certain lawyer" was led by the Holy Spirit to feel the deep need to know how he could identify who he should treat with "Love." The "certain lawyer" must then be seen as oneself needing, "desiring, wishing, wanting, willing, designing and ready" (from Strong's usage and HELPS Word-studies of "*theló*") to "regard oneself as righteous" (from "*dikaiōsai heauton*"). One cannot fulfil the intent of the Law without knowing who God commanded all His followers to "Love."

It is at this point that Jesus responded to that important question relative to defining "a neighbor" by telling the parable known as the Good Samaritan. In this, and in all parables told by Jesus, it is important to see him speaking the truth, as all holy Scripture is the Word of God and the truth is always being told. Because a parable is told in a 'make believe' or hypothetical setting, with characters that seem to be fictitious, a parable can be viewed as veering away from literal truth, entering into the realm of symbolic truth.

Parables Explained: The Parable of the Good Samaritan

Parables should then be taken as metaphor, which is truth that is told by example. What might or might not have happened, exactly as told, becomes understood as irrelevant as the point of the story is to address a theological issue that had presented itself to Jesus. The answer is then the truth of God being told by His Son, related to known concepts, accepted positions, and typical scenarios that the Jewish people readily recognized. However, every parable told by Jesus should be seen with the caveat of it being a deeper truth, matching the depth of Holy Scripture.

Knowing that Jesus had just prayed to God, thanking Him for the success of his disciples that had been sent into ministry for Him and given the powers of the Holy Spirit to experience and use to promote the Will of God, one should remember Jesus saying, "You [Father] have hidden these things from the wise and learned, and revealed them to little children." A parable should be seen in the same way.

The parables of Jesus make him be a character that is the truth present in his answers to questions stemming from his ministerial presence in Judea and Galilee (and beyond). For this reason, one should look for the hidden presence of Jesus in a parable and see what role he plays in this truth told in a narrative designed for 'little children'. Therefore, to repeat the NIV translation in this segment, Jesus said in reply to the question about who a neighbor was:

> "A man was going down from Jerusalem to Jericho, when he was attacked by robbers. They stripped him of his clothes, beat him and went away, leaving him half dead. A priest happened to be going down the same road, and when he saw

the man, he passed by on the other side. So too, a Levite, when he came to the place and saw him, passed by on the other side. But a Samaritan, as he traveled, came where the man was; and when he saw him, he took pity on him. He went to him and bandaged his wounds, pouring on oil and wine. Then he put the man on his own donkey, brought him to an inn and took care of him. The next day he took out two denarii and gave them to the innkeeper. 'Look after him,' he said, 'and when I return, I will reimburse you for any extra expense you may have.'" (Luke 10:30-35)

In this parable, the story is easy to follow and the Greek text is basically the same, with only a few elements where the translation misses what needs to be pointed out. As with every symbolic statement, it should be grasped that nothing is told without intent by God. It must be understood that God is telling the story through His Son, who only spoke the Will of the Father. When one realizes that everything is spoken with deeper purpose, it should make one listen (or read) this parable slowly, pondering the depth of everything said.

First, where we read "A man," the Greek of Luke states, "*Anthrōpos tis*," which is once again the reference to "A man certain." This should be read as identifying "The man" as a Jew and not simply another "man." The capitalization of "*Anthrōpos*" makes this as an important human being that is descended from Adam and the other Patriarchs of Israel. In this sense, the "Man" can be seen as Jesus, as a Jew walking the path of righteousness that this parable addresses. That doubly makes him be identified as "certain," being known among all his disciples (who were all Jews).

Parables Explained: The Parable of the Good Samaritan

Second, it should be grasped historically how the road to Jericho was a rather desolate stretch of land that passed between ridges of the Judean Hills (the Central Highlands of modern Israel), which ran from Samaria, to the north, to the Judean Desert, to the southeast of Jerusalem. Those hills spread eastward to the Jordan plain, with Jericho closer to the hill than the river's edge (due to seasonal flooding). The elevation difference between the Temple Mount [3,800 feet above sea level] and Jericho [800 feet below sea level] meant a descent when traveling east and an ascent when traveling west. Atop the Adummim ridge (or pass) overlooking Jericho was a Roman fort. There security forces kept watch over the route, and that was where the inn would have been located.

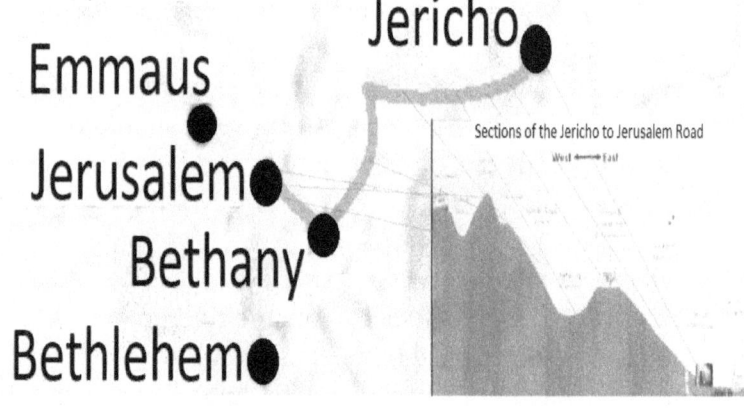

Elevation graphic gained from William Schlegel video presentation, as presented by Rick Yohn Ministries.org.

Between Jerusalem and Jericho was barren wilderness, where the Roman soldiers could not police it or make it safe for travel alone. The Canyon of Nahal Og was where the Wadi Og cut a route of water runoff that headed to the

Dead Sea and could have been a place where some pools of water and caves made it possible for bandits to stay in hiding, approximately half-way between Jerusalem and Jericho. Steep roads were the only ways out of the canyon. Such a place would be out of view of the Roman forts and a prime place for predatory attacks on travelers. Safety, therefore, was done by travelling in groups, or else small groups or individuals would become easy prey to predators that would watch for opportunities. This is then the danger of a lost sheep entering a realm of that was known for being where dangerous wolves had their dens.

Third, when Jesus said, "They stripped him of his clothes, beat him and went away," this should be seen as how an enemy will treat somebody. This is then in line with when Jesus said during his Sermon on the Mount:

> "You have heard that it was said, 'Love your neighbor and hate your enemy.' But I tell you, love your enemies and pray for those who persecute you, that you may be children of your Father in heaven. He causes his sun to rise on the evil and the good, and sends rain on the righteous and the unrighteous." (Matthew 5:43-45, NIV)

This reminder makes the onset of "robbers" be parallel to their acts of persecution, where it would be doubtful that Jews would hide in the wilderness to attack other Jews. The Greek word "*lēstais*" translates as "robbers," but is synonymous with "bandits" (Strong's usage) and "unscrupulous marauders that did not hesitate from using violence." (HELPS Word-studies) Just prior to Jesus making this announcement, he had said, relative to "an eye for an eye, a tooth for a tooth," "If anyone wants to sue

Parables Explained: The Parable of the Good Samaritan

you and take your shirt, hand over your coat as well." That presented a legal way for Jews to attack Jews, where it was neighbor against neighbor. The aspect of violent attackers "stripping one of clothes and beating one physically," while symbolically having the same effects as the damage that lawsuits bring, the use of physical force speaks clearly of the rage of emotions within enemies that one has to face from time to time.

Fourth, when Luke wrote that Jesus said the robbers departed the "certain Man" "leaving him half dead," this makes his use of the words "*aphentes hēmithanē*" worth closer inspection. The Greek word "*aphentes*" is a aorist active participle verb, meaning "leaving" is too present tense to be an accurate translation. Instead, it can mean "having left," with the masculine nominative implying "having left [him]." This then appears to relate to the "robbers," but the comma separates this segment from the prior one-word statement, "*apēlthon*," meaning "went away." With that more directed to the departure of the attackers, "having left" should be viewed in more spiritual terms, relative to "him" the "certain Man," such that "having left half-dead" is a statement about a lesson focusing on "eternal life," versus mortal death and reincarnation.

This means seeing the parable as coming from the Christ Mind and not something totally off the top of Jesus' head (brain action), everything has deeper meaning that can be brought to the surface with reflection and meditation, praying for God's guidance. In this sense, "*aphentes*" says, "having sent away, having left alone, having permitted to depart, and having let suffer," where Jesus was sent to the Jews, "left alone" for them to welcome or reject. This means the story told in the presence of Jesus' disciples was prophesying his own treatment, which included harassment, spies in his camp and threats to have him stoned to death for doing the Lord's work on a Sabbath.

The Greek word "*hēmithanē*" clearly translates as "half dead," as a combined form word from "*hémisus*" ("half") and "*thnéskó*" ("dead"). (NAS Exhaustive Concordance, word origin) What needs to be intuited from this is "half dead" also means "half alive." While the focus on one being near death appears as a traumatic state of being and is the surface design of the parable's storyline, that misses the repeating theme in the teachings of Jesus that mortal life is death, requiring God's salvation to avoid that end. It is then this one word that takes the "lawyer's" question about "eternal life" and begins a story of one who is not dead from being a mortal, but only "half dead" because he has been sent by the Father, in a human body that is bound to die, but sent with the Holy Spirit within him, which makes his eternal soul be granted eternal life after death. Thus, the attackers are prophesying the plot to have Jesus killed, but his recovery in the end of the parable prophesies his resurrection.

Fifth, the Greek word "*hiereus*" translates as "priest," but the NIV translation avoids identifying this as a Jewish "priest." It is an assumption but not directly stated in their translation. In the Greek of Luke, he is identified by the use of the word "*tis*," making him be "a priest certain." Because the basic word "priest" is stated, the word can mean "one who offers sacrifice to a god" (Strong's definition), which many Gentile religions (like that of the Romans) had. Undoubtedly, Roman holy men were sent to the frontier to be along with Roman soldiers in order to make sacrifices to their many gods and make their troops feel

Parables Explained: The Parable of the Good Samaritan

protected. The use of "certain" lets the read know the word "priest" means one who was deemed "sacred because of belonging to the Temple." (HELPS Word-studies)

When one sees how this "priest" would "see, look upon, experience, and/or beware" the one who was "half dead" and "pass by on the other side," assumptions are made that visualize what Jesus said. The listener or reader sees a beaten man lying on the side of the road in the dirt, nearly dead from attack wounds. Probably, one imagines a rather wide and flat dirt road, where a body is obviously crumpled up on the ground at one side of this road, so it is easy to pass by this man on the other side. While the story is designed to convey that imagery, the words written by Luke speak on a deeper level.

By Jesus identifying a "certain priest," meaning a "priest" of the Temple in Jerusalem, one who routinely used a dagger to slaughter animals to be burned on the altar, this is a clear statement that the "priest" was not afraid of seeing a little blood. He was capable of taking a live creature and killing it. Perhaps he even experienced times when the workload was so great he made an inaccurate throat slice, leaving an animal "half dead," causing him to make another cut to put it out of its misery. This means when "he passed by on the opposite side," the "priest" was showing no compassion for the man that was "half dead." (Thayer's Greek Lexicon analysis of this usage in Luke 10:31) Still, this is an incomplete view as to the meaning.

The common scholarly view of this moving "to the other side" is that a Temple "priest" would have this course of movement mandated by law. The Jews had rites of purification that meant any contact with blood or a corpse would make them impure. This, of course, is not written into the storyline but assumed to have been readily understood by the disciples of Jesus, knowing the rituals of "priests" as quite demanding of cleanliness. The "Pharisees and teachers of the law" confronted Jesus about his disciples picking grains from the field and eating them without first washing their hands. (Matthew 15:1-2) However, Jesus pointed out how inconsistent those Jews were at being totally observant of the law, quoting Isaiah:

> "These people honor me with their lips, but their hearts are far from me. They worship me in vain; their teachings are merely human rules" (Matthew 15:8-9, NIV, from Isaiah 29:13)

This means the assumption that a "certain priest" "passed by on the opposite side [of the road]" due to his fearing becoming unclean from contact with a bloody person, "seen" in a "half dead" state, misses the truth hidden beneath what is actually stated. Closer inspection is required to find the hidden truth, rather than depend on what the surface seems to imply.

While this verse implies "the other side" was "the road" the "priest happened" to be traveling, the word "*antiparēlthen*" does not clearly state that. The Greek word "*hodō*," meaning "road," was stated prior to a comma mark that appears in mid-verse. It is that comma mark that separates the use of "road" from "he passed by on the other side" ("*antiparēlthen*"). This make "*hodō*" become more than simply the road to Jericho from Jerusalem, but "a way, road, journey, path" that "certain" men travel, in order to reach "eternal life." A "certain priest" was then a committed Jew that was consecrated to perform tasks in the

Parables Explained: The Parable of the Good Samaritan

Temple, as a "road" that was expected to lead him to please Yahweh. This means "he passed by on the other side" as a Jew who served the Lord differently than the "certain Man" that was in a body of flesh guaranteed eternal life. Thus, the "priest" was a dead man walking.

To fully grasp this intent, one has to see the combined form state of the Greek word "*hēmithanē*," as "half dead," now being mirrored in another combined form word – "*antiparēlthen*." The word "*antiparēlthen*" is formed by combining the Greek word "*anti*" with the word "*parerchomai*." While this can certainly translate as meaning "opposite pass by," or imply "he passed by on the opposite side," there are other possibilities that should be realized. This is because two words written by a prophet of God (in this case Luke writing "*hēmithanē*" followed by "*antiparēlthen*") are making a statement of symmetry, which is an important sign to follow for deeper awareness.

The Greek word "*anti*" is said to be defined as, "over against, opposite, instead of" (Strong's definition), with its usage implying: "(a) instead of, in return for, over against, opposite, in exchange for, as a substitute for, (b) on my behalf, (c) wherefore, because." (Strong's usage) The figurative meaning is then said to be, by HELPS Word-studies: "in place of," i.e. what substitutes (serves as an equivalent, what is proportional)."

The Greek word "*parerchomai*" is said to be defined as, "to pass by, to come to" (Strong's definition), with its usage implying: "I pass by, pass away, pass out of sight; I am rendered void, become vain, neglect, and disregard." Thayer's Greek Lexicon states this word metaphorically means: "to pass away, perish; to neglect, omit; and to be led by, to be carried past, be averted."

When these two words are reconsidered in a combined form translation, where the "path" or "road" is no longer necessary to limit its scope, one can see that a relationship to "half dead" (alternatively "half alive") is the "certain priest" was "a substitute for disregard." Instead of travel the way of righteousness, as a "certain priest," he was ensuring he would "pass away in return for" his way of 'life', which ensured mortal death and reincarnation. Instead of gaining "half-life," he ensured "total death" by "vainly walking on his own behalf."

Sixth, Jesus then introduced "a Levite," where the capitalized Greek word "*Leuitēs*" is written. There is no use of "*tis*," as the proper name then becomes a statement of one that is of the Tribe of Levi, thus a descendant of Aaron, the first High Priest of the Israelites. The scholars see the "Levite" as somewhat confusing, when a "priest" was known to have to avoid direct contact with corpses (even though he saw a man "half dead") a "Levite" was recognized as an assistant to a priest, on a "lower-level of priesthood." (Bible Odyssey.org) They were said to "man the temple gates, clean the temple, slaughter some of the sacrificial animals, and perform the music during temple worship (as from 1Chr 23-25)." (Bible Odyssey.org) Therefore, the confusion is from wondering why one of the Temple who was not forbidden from handling a corpse or one with bloody wounds "passes by on the other side".

This should be addressed on two levels of inspection. First, the capitalization makes the "Levite" be of greater importance than the one identified simply as a "certain priest," due to the capitalization. The "priest" had an excuse to walk by as one filled with apathy, due to having interpreted the Law as being an excuse for not caring about anyone other than himself. The "Levite," on the other hand, is not so excused and more importantly should have been filled with compassion for having seen anyone (Jew or Gentile) in a state that was in need of attention. This means the importance is not from a "Levite" being an integral part of the Temple, but rather the importance comes as the name being synonymous with every Jew in the return from exile. Whereas the "priest" was lower-case as an indication of God having told Nathan to tell David he did not need a permanent building to be kept in, the "Levite" was supposed to be the ones dedicated to doing priestly duties in all places where the Israelites lived. The answer to why the "Levite" was used as an example by Jesus it that name sets up two types of Jews. This becomes clear when another capitalized word is observed deeply.

That word in Greek is "*Homoiōs*," which the NIV translations shows as "So too." The word more accurately is defined as meaning "likewise, in like manner" (Strong's definition), with the intent in usage to be read-heard as: "similarly, in the same way, equally." (Strong's usage) When the capitalization is then making a statement of importance, the "Levite" is then following the same "path" as the Temple "priest." That becomes a statement that the Jews who assisted the Temple "priests," but were free to act independently of them, they acted "Likewise" or "Equally." This becomes an important statement of fear. Whereas the "priest" could readily walk a different route without any compassion for who was left in his wake, the "Levite" feared not doing the same, which was a sign that he was filled with a desire to help, but felt forced to act as the Temple would. The fear would be from banishment or rejection; and that makes the "certain Man" become an example of one outcast from the Temple, regardless of that being right or wrong. As the "Levite" walked a "road" to ruin (death), he felt deep guilt from doing so, meaning the visual should show him scurry along at a faster rate, wanting his sin to quickly pass behind him.

Seventh, Jesus next introduced "A Samaritan" to the parable. It is imperative to understand what that means. According to Thayer's Greek Lexicon says of a Samaritan:

> "i.e.: an inhabitant either of the city or of the province of Samaria. The origin of the Samaritans was as follows: After Shalmaneser (others say Esarhaddon, cf. Ezra 4:2, 10; but see Kautzsch in Herzog edition 2, as referred to under the preceding word), king of Assyria, had sent colonists from Babylon, Cuthah, Ava, Hamath, and Sepharvaim into the land of Samaria which he had devastated and depopulated, those Israelites who had remained in their desolated country (cf. 2 Chronicles 30:6, 10; 2 Chronicles 34:9) associated and intermarried with these heathen colonists and thus produced a mixed race. When the Jews on their return from exile were preparing to rebuild the temple of Jerusalem, the Samaritans asked to be allowed to bear their part in the common work. On being refused by the Jews, who were unwilling to recognize them as brethren, they not only sent letters to the king of Persia and caused the Jews to be compelled to desist from their undertaking flown to the second year of Darius (Hystaspis), but also built a temple for themselves on Mount Gerizim, a place held sacred even from the days of Moses (cf. Deu-

Parables Explained: The Parable of the Good Samaritan

> teronomy 27:12, etc.), and worshipped Jehovah there according to the law of Moses, recognizing only the Pentateuch as sacred. This temple was destroyed by John Hyrcanus. Deprived of their temple, the Samaritans have nevertheless continued to worship on their sacred mountain quite down to the present time, although their numbers are reduced to some forty or fifty families. Hence, it came to pass that the Samaritans and the Jews entertained inveterate and unappeasable enmity toward each other.

From this well-stated history that explains the "inveterate and unappeasable enmity" that the Jews of Jerusalem (influencing those throughout Judea and Galilee) had towards the Samaritan people, one should grasp how by Jesus simply saying "A Samaritan" would immediately conjure up feelings of anger in the Jews listening to him tell a parable. One must then be able to identify "A Samaritan" as an "enemy" of all Jews, more so than Gentiles like the Romans were.

While Samaria was the province between Galilee and Judea, through which all pilgrimages to Jerusalem would regularly take Jews, the region was under Roman control and open hostilities among the mixed races would not be tolerated without forceful intervention. Thus, the story of Jesus and the Samaritan woman at the well in Samaria, where the disciples would have been appalled to find Jesus speaking to her because she was Samaritan, it should be realized that this "enemy" of the Jews was avoided as much as possible. Encounters were inevitable but disdain seethed inwardly nonetheless.

Form understanding this typical view of Samaritans by the disciples of Jesus, that inner anger should be seen as offset by Jesus saying the "Samaritan took pity," when "he saw" the condition of "a Man half dead." It is this inner feeling of "pity" that needs to be seen as not being an automatic, pre-programmed response to another human being. It is not a programmed response to show pity because of bad teachings that make people "enemies," without any direct relationship ever having been established between one and another. Therefore, the "certain priests" had created this concept of "enemies," which the "Levites" learned and ran with, living accordingly; they "passed by on the other side" of anyone who did not meet their interpretation of who, what, when, and where was acceptable, with the 'why' being analysis that removed pity and compassion from the mix.

The Greek word written by Luke is "*esplanchnisthē*," which is the aorist passive tense, dependent indicative voice, third person singular of "*splagchnizomai*," meaning, "he was moved in the inward parts" or "he felt compassion." (Strong's definition) By translating "he took pity," the intent of the usage is "he was moved" emotionally. (Strong's usage) When the definition of "pity" is understood to mean "a feeling of sorrow and compassion caused by the suffering and misfortunes of others," it should be seen how "sorrow, compassion, and pity" are inner feeling that are caused by one's ability to realize how the suffering and misfortune of others is no different than that which causes the same traumas within oneself. It is the truth of sympathy.

When the Samaritan is to be compared to the "priest" and the "Levite," it is important to realize that all three saw a man that was obviously in a state of "suffering and misfortune," causing each man to be emotionally "moved" in some inner way. The "priest" was moved intellectually and reacted as his education had trained him: He avoided direct contact with someone who might die. The "Levite" was "Likewise" emotionally "moved inwardly," but he had no education that led him to avoidance. It was fear that motivated him to avoid any direct contact with someone "suffering" from "misfortune." He felt going near one in pain would cause him pain as well.

In all three encounters, none of those travelers knew what religious beliefs the man that was "half dead" held. That is not part of the storyline, meaning the Samaritan was "moved inwardly" to stop and help a human being in need, regardless of the "inveterate and unappeasable enmity" that existed between Samaritans and Jews. The Samaritan man "was moved in the inward parts" because he would want someone to "Likewise" be filled with compassion, should the same suffering and misfortune befall him. Therefore, one must see the Samaritan as an example of "Do unto others as you would have them do unto you." (Matthew 7:12 and Luke 6:31)

Relative to seeing Jesus as the "Man" to whom God sent only to the lost children of Israel, this statement about the "Samaritan" coming upon Jesus should be deeply understood, which comes by a slow analysis of the written text. While the "Levite" was not identified as "certain" (from the Greek "*tis*") and the "priest" was, making them (along with "a Man certain") be Jews by birth and position, the Samaritan is so identified in a separate segment of words that state "*tis hodeuōn*," or "certain journeying" or "certain traveling." The use of "*tis*" makes the "road" or "path" representative of the same religious "way" being traveled by everyone in the parable. While not a Jew (not a certain "Samaritan"), the "Samaritan" is "certain" as a child of Israel – the name of the Patriarch Jacob and the Northern Kingdom.

Next, the following segment of words is translated as "came where the man was." More than a simple statement of action in a parable, the Greek text states "*ēlthen kat' auton*" or "came to him." As a separate statement, where only these three word have meaning that is divine, detached from any of the other words surrounding them for a moment of deep pondering, the "journey" that is the "road traveled" is that direction preached by Moses: "to come to God." That is both a quest for eternal life in heaven and a realization of God within, as inward feelings that motivate and lead one in the "path" walked. This then reconnects to the words surrounding as a metaphoric statement that "a Samaritan came to Jesus," and was overwhelmed emotionally because he was not total death (a mortal of no Spirit); Jesus was only "half dead" and offered the promise of eternal life.

The NIV shows a semi-colon mark, followed by the two phrases: "and when he saw him, he took pity on him." The Greek of Luke states this as one phrase, beginning with the word "*kai*." Following after is written, "*idōn esplanchnisthē*" or "having seen was moved with compassion." The "*kai*" says this emotional change in the "Samaritan" was of great importance, as it was important for the "Samaritan" to "experience, perceive, discern and beware" what Jesus offered to all "certain" followers of religion honoring YHWH. What was "seen" that "caused deep inner feelings to move" him was viewed through Spiritual insight, not human vision.

The eighth point comes when verse 34 is read as how the "Samaritan" acted after having come to Jesus, as depicted in "a Man half dead." We read in the NIV translation, "He went to him and bandaged his wounds, pouring on oil and wine. Then he put the man on his own donkey, brought him to an inn and took care of him." This paints a clear picture of the "Samaritan" doing good works, as he took the time and gave freely of his own to help another individual in need. That surface meaning is a necessary part of the apparent parable. However, there is an underlying story being told that parallels the life of Jesus, as it pertained to his disciples who would become Apostles.

To see this depth appear, one has to slow down the reading process and refer to the Greek text, where punctuation and marker words enhance the text presented. The Greek text here breaks this into five segments, based on the presence of commas and a semi-colon, with the presence of "*kai*" found several times. The verse's first segment begins with the word "*kai*" and it is importantly placed within two other segments. The five segments should be read metaphorically as steps in one's ministry, described as follows (using a literal translation into English, which differs from the NIV translation):

> 1."***kai*** having consented" – This segment importantly places focus on the "Samaritan having drawn near" to Jesus, where this "approach" can only be done by one being willing to sacrifice self for the betterment of others. This is the "coming to Jesus" truth, which is sacrifice of self so Jesus can be resurrected within one's being. This is baptism by the Holy Spirit and

receiving the Christ Mind.

2. "he bound up the wounds of him" – This as a separate segment of words does not bring an inference that "of him" (from the Greek "*auton*") is anyone specific. The literal evidence points away from "him" being "a Man." The pronoun implies "himself" or "the same" person. This realization allows the third person of "*katedēsen*" ("he bound up") not be the "Samaritan." This means the presence of the Holy Spirit is what bandages the wounds of life's scars and pains.

3. "pouring oil **kai** wine" – This is the anointment of a high priest <u>in the name of Jesus Christ,</u> where "oil" (from the Greek "*elaion*") figuratively means "the indwelling (empowering) of the Holy Spirit." (HELPS Word-studies). The insertion of "*kai*" then separates this anointment so sole focus is placed on "wine" (from the Greek "*oinon*"), which metaphorically means having become the "blood of Christ." The importance stated in "**kai** wine" says the Holy Spirit cursed through the Samaritan's body of flesh in the same way fermented grapes make one tingle all over.

4. "having placed indeed now himself on the basis of condition personal yoke" – This is a statement of self-sacrifice as a servant of the Lord, where one willingly foregoes selfish desires and pleasure, just as a donkey or a mule waits for its master to next put it to use, knowing the master will care for the "beast" properly. This is then a statement about one's willing commitment (a personal Covenant written on one's heart) to be subject to God's Will.

> 5. "he led him towards a public house for the reception of strangers [Thayer's Greek Lexicon for "inn" or "*pandocheion*"] **kai** took care of him" – Here the pronoun "he" becomes God, as a reborn Christ, who has married with one's soul and leads the body of flesh (becoming also "half dead") into synagogues or churches of Christians to preach. It also states that the body is "led towards" becoming an "inn" for the Christ Mind to lodge, such that the House of the Lord is always meant to be as mobile as was the Ark of the Covenant. A **Christ**ian becomes the truth of a church, just as wherever two or more gather <u>in my name</u>, then Jesus will be there. Unlike "priests" who have to pour over books and notes to prepare a sermon based on intellectual research of facts and accepted theories, one who is Jesus Christ reborn will be cared for by the Holy Spirit and the words will flow forth from an Apostles in the same they flowed from Jesus.

The ninth point then surfaces from verse 35 from doing the same deeper inspection of the text. That verse is simply translated by the NIV as stating, "The next day he took out two denarii and gave them to the innkeeper. 'Look after him,' he said, 'and when I return, I will reimburse you for any extra expense you may have.'"

This seemingly two sentences breaks down into seven segments of words, all separated by comma marks, where each segment makes a separate 'sentence' that needs to be understood separately from the others. Within those are three uses of "*kai*," with two of those beginning a statement (indicating the statement is important), with one of those capitalized. Also, there appear two words that are set off by "<<" and ">>" marks, while immediately followed by a double arrow ("<=>"), also known as a leftrightarrow. The use of these marks is not shown in the NIV translation. Therefore, these seven segments should be read as free-standing 'sentences' that join to form a 'paragraph'.

> 1."***Kai*** at condition fresh" – The capitalized use of "*Kai*" indicated a most important transition point, which then relates back to the segment prior, in verse 34, which was a state of being where God was leading an Apostle, or "taking care of him." This means "*Kai*" begins by acknowledging that new state of being, where one is no longer responsible for his or her acts, because of having submitted fully to the guidance of the Holy Spirit. This makes the translation of "the next day" be properly read as a "fresh" start. (Strong's Exhaustive Concordance)

> 2."having cast out <<two small amounts of silver>> <=>" – The use of arrow marks is a way of separating the words "*dyo dēnaria*" from the word "*ekbalōn*," making "two denarii" be read as an aside, rather than a direct statement. Because this aside acts as interjection into a flow of thought, the double arrow (<=>) becomes a mark that tells one to read it as a link to the first word of the following segment of words to the word "*ekbalōn*," which translates best as "having cast out."

> In mathematic statements by symbols found in Greek, the leftrightarrow indicates a state of equivalence, such that "if A then B," with the truth of A being equal to the truth of B. (Wikipedia "List of math-

ematical symbols") This then means A is based on "having cast out" and B is then the equation of "he gave" (from "*edōken,*" the lead word following the leftrightarrow). The interjection is then relative to "having cast out," but more a reflection back to the "fresh" start an Apostle experiences when led by the Holy Spirit.

This means that "two" is not a number of "denarii," but the "two" that have been joined in marriage: God and a soul trapped in human flesh. This means the use of "denarii," which meant "ten asses" or "ten amounts of silver" that was generally a day's wages for a Roman soldier, becomes metaphor for "metal" of value. Because the soul and the Holy Spirit are joined (two as one), the connection should now be seen metaphysically as by a "silver" cord. Such a spiritual cord has been reported by those who have become "half dead," leaving their bodies of flesh for some period of time, before being resurrected. They report that this "silver" cord being severed means the soul can no longer return and exist in that body of flesh. Therefore, with this deep meaning seen set apart by special marks, "having cast out" demons from influencing the soul, "two" have created a bond of purity and value that gets one through the costs of each day.

3. "he gave condition host ***kai*** brought word" – The third person singular form of the aorist verb "*didómi*" means "he gave," which references back to "having cast out" (due to the link formed by the double arrow), making "he" be God and His Holy Spirit "given." This should be seen in the light of Paul's letters,

where he wrote of the "gifts" of the Holy Spirit being "given" (Greek "*didotai*"). The word "*pandochei*," which does translate commonly to "innkeeper," is now seen relative to the word being read as "host." This makes the body of flesh and its naturally placed soul (by God at birth) be the "host" body that God married, via His Holy Spirit. It flashes one back to verse 34, where "inn" was translated as "public house for the reception of strangers," and makes an Apostle be the representation of a church that welcomes strangers, as an "inn" that houses God's Christ. Following the importance indicated by the word "*kai*" is the powerful statement that that "given" by "having cast out" the interference of human brains is the "Word" (given artificial capitalization by the use of "*kai*") spoken by Apostles.

4."Attend to oneself" – The use of the Greek pronoun "*autou*" is again a reference to the "self" as the "same" one reading or hearing the words. The Greek word "*Epimelētheti*" is capitalized, giving great importance to the act of "Caring," The act of what the Holy Spirit speaks through an Apostle is then "brought word" or "said" with divine wisdom as a command (in the imperative mood) to "Take care!" It comes from one who speaks from experience, "Having taken care of oneself," as a teaching to others.

5."*kai* that certain possibility you might spend in addition" – This becomes a statement of the costs that taking care of oneself will incur. The introduction by the word "*kai*" makes this importantly state an expectation to expend more than first spent in the transition that sacrificed self-ego, in exchange for the Holy

Spirit and the Christ Mind. The cost of redemption is an ongoing sacrifice.

6. "I with condition returning" – This begins with the Greek word "*egō*," which not only says "I" or "me" but is a statement about the self-ego, which has to be sacrificed in order to "Attend to oneself." This is then "I" being a statement of the presence of God, as Jesus reborn within the flesh of another, creating the "condition" of "I" being "with" the Holy Spirit. This is a confirmation of "two" being linked by "silver," the cord of Christ. The use of the Greek word "*epanerchesthai*" (as "coming back" or "returning") is then the promise made by Jesus to his disciples that he would be "returning." His "return" is his resurrection in an Apostle (being <u>in the name of Jesus Christ</u>), with his "returning" having occurred many times over in the advent of Christianity.

7. "I will restore you." – This is the promise of eternal life, where the cost of admission to Heaven is the absolution of past sins and the wearing of the robes of righteousness forevermore, upon the time one is filled with the Holy Spirit and transformed into the rebirth of the Son of God as another Son of Man (regardless of one's human gender). This is the truth behind the statement that confesses, "We believe in one baptism for the forgiveness of sins," as the sacrifice of self-ego, to resurrect Jesus Christ within one's being, means the baptism that marries God with one's soul forever, with physical water paying absolutely no role in this restoration.

This lesson has given ample evidence to show the verbiage

of Luke is clearly telling two stories with the same words, with one appearing to be fictitious and the other clearly (from our perspective two millennia later) being the truth of Jesus Christ. The story told to the "lawyer" is perceived as being heard with ears like those sitting in the pews in Christian churches whenever this parable is read aloud, where the fantasy of a parable is the only meaning grasped. However, one must see how the "lawyer," most likely someone like Joseph of Arimathea (if not him specifically), heard Jesus speak and was led by the Holy Spirit to grasp all the nuisances of his words and fully comprehend the intended meaning via the Holy Spirit. After all, he had just been moved earlier to speak the truth of the Holy Spirit, leading him to then ask Jesus to explain who a "neighbor" was.

It should be noted that Jesus could have continued the parable and added information about the recovery of the "certain Man" (known to be a Jew) and the return of the "Samaritan" to the "inn." The story could have reached a fairy tale-like happy ending, where the two men from two camps, with "inveterate and unappeasable enmity toward each other," were to become good friends forevermore. Instead, Jesus ended the story where he did and asked the "lawyer," "Which of these three do you think was a neighbor to the man who fell into the hands of robbers?"

Because the "lawyer" answered Jesus, saying, "The one who had mercy on him," the answer was not based on the flawed logic of preconceptions and bias. As a "lawyer," one who owed his position of authority to his close association with those who ruled the Second Temple, to denounce a Temple "priest" and a "Levite," by omission, could not have been an answer easily given without having seen the deeper truth. The "lawyer" did not say, "The Samaritan," as that identification did nothing to show the true Spirit of the man himself. To point out the "compassion" (or "pity" or "mercy") a human being had towards another means the "lawyer" felt that as he listened to Jesus' words. Therefore, the "lawyer" did not simply give Jesus the answer he wanted him to say, as he was led to see the truth and realize the answer to "who my neighbor is" is relative to all who serve God, as demonstrated by acts that speak of His presence within.

The question posed by Jesus, as recorded by Luke in his thirty-sixth verse of this chapter (ten), actually was not directed to anyone specifically. Knowing that both Jesus and the "lawyer" were standing during this lesson in parable, assuming the rest of the disciples (over seventy) were seated and listening, the question was made to everyone present. As it was a question coming from Jesus' mouth, being one sent through him by the Father to the Son, the question is just as pertinent to everyone reading these verses or hearing them read aloud in a church today. It asks us, individually, to answer the question, "Who is my neighbor," based on the words spoken by Jesus.

The answer to that question should be the same as that given by the "lawyer," as all true Christians who are filled with God's Holy Spirit are likewise "experts in the Law," because God's Law is written in the hearts of those with true faith (beyond simple belief). By realizing this, it is then worthwhile to know that Luke did not write, "The expert in the law replied," as the NIV presumes. Instead, his words say "*Ho de eipen*," which literally translates to say, "Condition indeed now he said."

Here, again, the small untranslatable article "*ho*" is translated as "Condition," which is also the translations presented from "*to*" and variations of what seems to be the article stating "a, an, the." The capitalization must force one to see the deeper purpose, such that "Circumstance," "Experience," Cause," or "Condition" [all translations found for the same word elsewhere in New Testament Scripture, as listed by the NASB] represent an important "Condition" having been reached by all that will truthfully answer, "The one who showed compassion" is my neighbor.

The translation of the tiny Greek word "*de*" as "indeed now," rather than a simple conjunction stating "and" or "but," makes the question answered be just as timely then as it is at all subsequent times. To place a timeframe as "indeed now" or "on top of this, next, however" (HELPS Word-studies) says the "Condition" is relative to the time one has an epiphany and reaches that 'aha moment' of dawning. That moment can only come when one allows the Holy Spirit to open one's eyes to the truth spoken and feel the truth in one's heart. That is the "next" thing following a "Condition" of servitude to God having been reached and self-sacrifice is done willingly and lovingly, in subjection to the Father.

The use of the Greek word "*eipen*" as the third person singular aorist active indicative form of "*eipon*" ["I say, I speak, I tell"], the third person cannot be limited to that "lawyer." Just as Jesus said, as translated here above, "he gave condition host ***kai*** brought word," the third person "he" was God and the use of "*eipen*" is translated as "brought word," which is God speaking through an Apostle [as the "Samaritan" was in the parable]. This means the same "Condition" has been met by everyone (past, present, and future) who hears or reads these words written by Luke

Parables Explained: The Parable of the Good Samaritan

and is inwardly moved to grasp the truth hidden within them ["(God has) hidden these things from the wise and learned, and revealed them to little children" – Luke 10:21]. The answer then given can be the same coming from all who will serve the Lord, as their hearts will have opened to receive the Holy Spirit.

When Jesus heard this answer given to him [by the "lawyer," by the other disciples listening, and by those today who see the truth revealed] the NIV says Jesus responded by saying, "Go and do likewise." This appears on the surface to be akin to what a quarterback says in the huddle, after a play has been called or spoken – "Ready? Break!" It reads as if the meeting of Jesus and his disciples was then adjourned and everyone was sent out into the world to do what they did after class was over. The only confusion there would have been if a student left the meeting asking himself, "Did Jesus just tell me to walk alone to Jericho and get beaten and robbed? Or did he just tell me to invite a Samaritan over for dinner?"

The truth becomes clear when the Greek text is realized to state: "*Poreuou **kai** sy poiei homoiōs*." By now, one should realize (without any ability to understand Greek) that a powerful one-word statement is made, based on the capitalization of one word that is followed by the word "*kai*." The word "*kai*" then introduces an important statement that joins to the one-word statement.

The powerful one-word statement not only says, "Go," but more importantly "Travel, Journey," and even more importantly "Die." Here, HELPS Word-studies says of "*poreuomai*": "properly, to transport, moving something from one destination (port) to another; (figuratively) to go or depart, emphasizing the personal meaning which is attached to reaching the particular destination." In the imperative mood, "*Poreuou*" is stating a command to all who will become God's Apostles (reborn as the Christ) to "Transform from your worship of self-ego to reach the destination of eternal life by opening your hearts to the Holy Spirit!" One has to see the power of one word spoken by God the Father as having this depth of truth hidden within its letters.

Following the "*kai*," the Greek literally translates to state, "yourself act equally." Jesus spoke directly to each individual listening, as "*sy*" is the second person singular of "you" (not a collective or global "you all"), where "yourself" is identifying what makes "you" you. The command is then to "act, make, cause, manufacture, and/or do" of "oneself" in a "like manner, similarly, the same way, and/or equally" as did the "Samaritan" in the parable. When one has heard the verbiage be less about a "Samaritan" and more about an Apostle of Jesus, reborn as the Christ and having been changed inwardly, then the command is to "follow me!" This is why the Gospels are followed by the book that sites "The Acts of the Apostles."

In this section that is under the heading "Parable of the Good Samaritan" it is important to realize the parable was told in response to a "lawyer" standing up to confront Jesus about what will guarantee a soul's admission into Heaven. Jesus responded with the Laws of Moses, which were the standards set by God for His chosen people. As the "lawyer's" question was relative to the Commandments of God, Jesus asked the legal expert what was his answer to his own question, based on the Torah. It is then vital to grasp how the "lawyer" did not give an educated answer, based on his intellectual expertise, because it is illogical for any scholar of Divine Word to give the answer that the "lawyer" gave. His answer was completely his openness to receive the answer he sought from God.

When that premise is understood and taken as a given, the one should see how the "lawyer" had experienced an epiphany simply by standing up and being so bold as to ask Jesus for an answer. His question acted as a prayer and his answer was coming from the voice of God that he willingly received. From receipt of an answer that was beyond his normal abilities of comprehension, the "lawyer" heard his answer and was moved to ask for more clarification. He heard himself say the way to eternal life was to "love his neighbor as himself." However, he did not intellectually know who was considered his neighbor, even though God said to Moses, "Do not seek revenge or bear a grudge against anyone among your people, but love your neighbor as yourself." (Leviticus 19:18)

This was a question that was debated then by scholars, philosophers and intellectuals [Temple priests], whose answers confounded the Jews, whose lives were dependent on the answers given to them [the "Levites"]. This means the confusion as to "who is my neighbors" has always been debatable, ever since God spoke that command to Moses. It is still debated today; but the reason is akin to the question and answer: If you have to ask then you'll never know.

It becomes very important to see how God had Moses free the Israelites from their slavery to a world that did not know YHWH - a diety who said to identify Him as "I Am That I Am." The Egyptians are then a reflection of everybody in the world, who routinely do worldly things and worship worldly gods. God had Moses take those who would commit to serving only the One God Yahweh and separate them from the rest of the world: the metaphor of wandering in a wilderness. This separation means none of the Commandments agreed to by the tribes of Israel apply to anyone else in the world. Simply by recognizing this selectivity it becomes easy to see how "enemies" and "neighbors" are all members of the same collective of those who committed their lives to serve YHWH. It makes the ever-present 'us vs. them' conflict be relative to the microcosm of faith, rather than the macrocosm of everyone in the world, where differences are standard.

The dictionary definition of "neighbor" is: "a person living near or next door to the speaker or person referred to." (Lexico.com, from Oxford) It should then be realized that Jews, then and now, try to live amongst one another in Jewish "neighborhoods," so they will be able to maintain this commandment, based on an intellectual definition of what a "neighbor" is. Thus, to a Jew a "neighbor" is another Jew, but to a Gentile (including those professing to be Christians in the United States of America) a "neighbor" can be any one of similar or different religious beliefs, including atheists and agnostics. That view is obviously missing the selectivity requirement, as nowhere did God say love everyone in the world.

If he had, thirty thousand Israelites, who were guilty of melting gold down to make a statue of a calf, would have been spared, as a lesson how to "love" those who try to subvert that new "road" God was sending His children down. That "road" was no different than the road between Jerusalem and Jericho, as the wilderness experience is a religious requirement. If God had envisioned "love" meaning nobody can ever be punished for doing wrong, then there never would have been need for an Exodus.

One must then see how the answer given by the "lawyer" surprised himself, causing him to ask for more divine explanation, so that he could comply with the Father's commandments. As such, his question was not to Jesus, but to God; the answer from Jesus was from his mouth, but sourced from God. The parable was then God speaking to all who were then and would forever listen to the words spoken, as recorded by Luke.

This makes the parable by Jesus be a story told on two levels simultaneously, as the normal way God always speaks, thus always present in Holy Scripture; thus always present in every parable told by Jesus. It becomes an example of Jesus having just said the marvel of God's presence in his disciples, those sent out in ministry without any diplomas or degrees of expertise, was their abilities to know what wise men are incapable of knowing. The "lawyer" was then an equal to all who listened then and who read or hear today, as one of the "little children" through whom the voice of God emits: "out of the mouths of babes." (Psalm 8:2 and Matthew 21:16)

The Parable of the Good Samaritan is told by God through Jesus as an answer to the "lawyer's" prayer to understand who a "neighbor" is. The words clearly separate the Jews from the mix, as far as representing those Jews who prayed to the Temple in Jerusalem for guidance. The metaphor of them passing by "a Man" in need says their "path" to eternal life keeps them so narrow-minded in focus that they would go out of their way to avoid a "come to Jesus meeting." That coming from the mouth of Jesus to Jews was a statement from God to beware walking the "road" of selfishness, as no Apostle of Mine will ever be so rewarded, simply by being born of pure blood that links one's maternal heritage to a male child of Israel (a known lineage to an earthly Tribe).

When Jesus then brought in a hated "Samaritan," saying he too followed a "certain journey" as did the "certain priest" and the "Levite," that identification brought to mind an "enemy" that lived in the land between Galilee and Judea, separate from the towns filled by Jews, thus anything other than a "neighbor." However, the surface story told makes it clear that it was the selfless acts of a man that cared for another that would define him as "neighbor," but the metaphor says that it was his same path to Yahweh that had filled him with God's Holy Spirit, because he was led to come to Jesus and willingly answered that call by God.

This means that a "neighbor" means more than intellectualizing "love" as something that is easily done by all human beings with hearts of fleshy muscle, which represent mortal life when beating and pumping blood through one's veins and arteries. Any human being can love and hate and be filled with every human emotion, which change every time the winds of emotion blow. God's "Love" is only possible in human beings that sacrifice their self-egos in subjection to the Lord. The human example of God's "Love" is Jesus. Therefore, to "love one's neighbor as oneself," oneself has to be reborn as Jesus in the Christ, meaning a "neighbor" is equally one resurrected as Jesus Christ that is in need.

By seeing this dawning that the "lawyer" and many of the other seventy-plus disciples who heard Jesus speak-

Parables Explained: The Parable of the Good Samaritan

ing (including Judas Iscariot and possibly Nicodemus, as those with ears that could not hear this meaning) as the first inkling that Christian is a greater level of commitment to Yahweh than ever before realized by the Jews, it means "Christian" is more than a branch of religion. All religions are merely philosophies with camps of human beings that have intellectually come to join as believers. This means the duality of all religions is no different than the duality of the divinity in Holy Scripture. On the highest level, all religions are good [remember this parable is a reflection on "Good"] in their ideologies, systems, philosophies, concepts, teachings, and theories. However, all religions are flawed if the individuals base their beliefs on the practices of a few, with the many allowed the freedom to fail to maintain those practices themselves.

This is the failure of the religions that fall under the heading of "Christianity," as the vast majority base their piety on belief that Jesus was the Christ, with only a few from the past (those called Saints) actually able to live up to the teaching of Jesus, so the rest are just along for the "tag, you're it" ride. This is the same failure of the "certain priest" and the "Levite," who both journeyed the same "road" expected to take them to the Promised Land of Heaven. Christians can be substituted in this parable with the same moral being reached at the ending. One has to become Jesus reborn to have the strength and determination to stop and care for Jesus. The "Condition" that affords eternal life is "self-sacrifice," with no desire, right, thought, or argument for anything material ever stopping one from helping another Christian in need (or helping one trying to become Christian reach that goal).

As long as leaders stand on soapboxes and proclaim an enemy is our neighbor and we are responsible for loving philosophies that preach hatred and disbelief in God Almighty, because "Jesus said so," the religion is on a road to ruin, just as the kingdoms of Israel and Judah were. It makes understanding "who is my neighbor" be like the lesson of Zen meditation. When one thinks one has reached nirvana, then one is not there. This is then the answer to the question being, "If you have to ask, then you'll never know."

Parables Explained: The Parable of the Good Samaritan

heaven and against you. I am no longer worthy to be called your son.' But the father said to his servants, 'Quick! Bring the best robe and put it on him. Put a ring on his finger and sandals on his feet. Bring the fattened calf and kill it. Let's have a feast and celebrate. For this son of mine was dead and is alive again; he was lost and is found.' So they began to celebrate.

Meanwhile, the older son was in the field. When he came near the house, he heard music and dancing. So he called one of the servants and asked him what was going on. 'Your brother has come,' he replied, 'and your father has killed the fattened calf because he has him back safe and sound.' The older brother became angry and refused to go in. So his father went out and pleaded with him. But he answered his father, 'Look! All these years I've been slaving for you and never disobeyed your orders. Yet you never gave me even a young goat so I could celebrate with my friends. But when this son of yours who has squandered your property with prostitutes comes home, you kill the fattened calf for him!'

'My son,' the father said, 'you are always with me, and everything I have is yours. But we had to celebrate and be glad, because this brother of yours was dead and is alive again; he was lost and is found.' (Luke 15:11-32)

After Jesus telling a parable about a man with one hundred sheep and a woman with ten silver coins, the key number here is "a man who had two sons." One hundred

Parables Explained: The Parable of the Prodigal Son

(numerologically) represents a one (as 1+0+0=1), as does ten (1+0=1), but here the number two offers the symbolism of duality (as all references to two do). Simply from this number we are being told to look for opposite aspects of one, as duality is the nature of everyone.

When this verse makes a statement about "a man who had two sons," it should not be thought that Jesus was making this story up off the top of his head. Jesus said, "I am in the Father and the Father is in me," (John 14:11, NIV) which means Jesus opened his mouth and sounded physically like Jesus sounded while speaking the Word of the Father. In everthing Jesus is written to have said, it was God speaking through his words. When God speaks, prophecy is spoken.

Knowing that; think about another story told by the Word of the Father through Moses: Genesis 4. There, we find a man (Adam, whose name basically means "Man") in that story who had two sons: Cain and Abel. Since the story is about sinners and redemption, read verses 12-33 with that parallel story in the back of one's mind. Cain and Abel are a reflection of the duality of Man, which is projected in the parable of Jesus.

The Cain and Abel story should not be singled out, however. There is close parallels that can be found in Abraham's story, where his two sons were Ishmael and Isaac. We also see similarities in this parable told by Jesus (especially when there is talk about a "share of the estate" is the same as a birthright given by a father to his eldest son.

Still, the translation that says the "younger one" makes this seem to veer one away from the Cain and Abel story, because Cain (the sinner) was the first-born of Adam. However, the Greek word "*neōteros*" is a comparative degree of "*néos*," which compares this son to the other as "new, fresh." (Strong's "B") That assessment then leads HELPS Word-studies to add: "new ("new on the scene"); recently revealed or "what was not there before" (TDNT), including what is recently discovered." While the word is often used as a comparison of siblings, where one is "younger" than another or others, it is important to see the Father as God (the common understanding), meaning His place is Heaven, in the ethereal realm, not of this world. Therefore, one son has been newly born into the physical world, as a soul inhabiting flesh anew.

A Roman Catholic page I found on the Internet, searching for "prodigal son," listed twelve things to realize about this parable in Scripture. While it addresses the father of the son is God, it then goes into the human aspect of a human (Jewish) father with two sons. The author put focus on this having the meaning to scribes and Pharisees, when hearing that a younger son demanded his share of the estate, would have made them aghast. The eldest of two sons would have expected to receive two-thirds of the father's possessions and holdings, with the younger getting one-third. That transforms "the Father" in the story into a wealthy Jew owning a large property.

The article then goes into how such a demand for an early inheritance would have been absurd and quickly leading to the response, "Wait till I'm dead my son." The author surmised the whole scenario Jesus began with would not have happened. That writer of an article for a Roman Catholic website then had eyes that saw God giving his younger son one-third of all He owned (a physical impossibility), when the son asked for it, as God's enormous generosity. That is faulty reasoning and must be ignored, because nothing is stated by Jesus (through Luke) that indicates what percentage (if any) "my share of the estate" is.

The view to behold is the younger son having been given life in a body of flesh and bones. To see the story beginning in heaven, as "the Father" is clearly understood to be Yahweh, should be seen as a birth, when a soul has been given by God to a physical body. Upon birth, it would be quite natural for all live born human beings to request: "Father, give me my share of the estate."

Here, the Greek word "*ousias*" has been translated as "estate," but the word means "property, wealth, substance" (Strong's), with "goods" being the King James translation. The word "goods" is equal to "possessions." By simply asking for "my share" or (more properly, from "*epiballon meros*") the "portion [falling to] me," the son was asking for nothing more than the Father's plan for His son that had been born into the world. A spiritual gift from God does not need to be divided, as if God had limits, based on the number of children He sired.

When the younger son is compared to Abel, with Adam his father, his "share" was to be a shepherd. That is symbolic of him being given a purpose to tend to the flocks of the father. Simply because the parable told by Jesus does not state anything about the elder son, or whether or not he had been also given a "share," the assumption made can be that of Cain's, who was given the land, with a purpose to bring fruits from the soil. This is then similar to the two sons of Isaac, where Esau and Jacob also had different purposes in their lives. We are told, "Esau became a skillful hunter, a man of the open country, while Jacob was content to stay at home among the tents." (Genesis 25:27) The conclusion that can then be drawn is to each his own, where differences are based on preferences, with all being part of God's master plan (not happenchance).

When we read the translation, "So he divided his property between them," there actually is nothing written that says "property." The Greek word "*bion*" is written, as to what was divided between two sons, and that word means, "manner of life; livelihood." (Strong's "B") This is then a statement of a division of "life" manifested, with the younger son being given a mortal body in which his eternal soul (life breath from God) would reside, with a special purpose. The elder son would live separately in the material realm, with his equally special purpose, just as did Cain and Abel and Esau and Jacob. Each had been given the same gift of life and a special purpose from God.

When the story has us read, "Not long after that, the younger son got together all he had, set off for a distant country and there squandered his wealth in wild living," this brings up an image of inherited possessions being heaped onto some cart, so the son can carry away spiritual possessions into a material world. The problem with that imagery is it is set up by an introduction that is a poor translation that says, "Not long after that."

The Greek words written are "*Kai met' ou pollas hēmeras*," which properly state, "And after not many days." While a sense of time is gathered from that direct translation, the concept of "days" is then simplified to a few (not many) periods of twenty-four hours. This concept of a short period of time misses the point of a division having been made, where God's purpose given to His son – as a birthright

Parables Explained: The Parable of the Prodigal Son

blessing – was so much (or so little) that it could be gathered together in some way over a short period of time. The symbolism of "days" is completely missed; and it is vital to grasp that meaning.

The Greek word "*hēmera*" means "day," as that "period from sunrise to sunset," when the sun is shining brightly. Just like numbers are important symbolic statements, "day" means more than the twelve hours each day the Jews recognized as not being nighttime. The deeper meaning of "day" (remembering that the Father was in Jesus, speaking these words through His Son Jesus) is the "light of God" or "God's illumination" of purpose in this son's "life." Therefore, this series of word segments does not begin by simply saying, "Not long after that," but instead begins by importantly [every capitalized *Kai* is a signal that great importance follows] saying, "**And** afterwards [following the birth of a soul into human flesh] not many periods of God's illumination of purpose" followed in this son's life.

It was that limited grasp of why the son was given life in a world that needed the light of God to shine upon it, due to the darkness the world represents. As mortals, all who are born with a life of purpose are born into a world of death that needs light; but that birth makes one easily fall asleep in the false illusion of "reality. the world presents. Therefore, the son gathered what goodness he could bear on his own soul, having left the Father behind in heaven.

With that inherited sense of doing good and living righteous – the teachings of religions – the son then traveled into a world that was quite distant from the heavenly realm. The son soon got caught up in all the trappings of a world built to promote sins. Still, to say he squandered his gift (from the Greek word "*dieskorpisen* ") is not fully realizing the language written. The Greek states, "**kai** *ekei dieskorpisen tēn ousian autou zōn asōtōs*," which is better stated as, "**and** there he wasted the wealth (substance given) to him prodigally."

The two words "*diaskorpizó*" and "*asótós*" state "he wasted, scattered, dispersed, or winnowed" and that he did so "wastefully, extravagantly, or prodigally," which is where the title of "prodigal son" comes. The onus that is placed on the younger son by this designation of his being identified as "extravagantly wasteful because of "loose living," i.e. a debauched, profligate lifestyle (Lk 15:13)" according to the information supplied by HELPS Word-studies, gives the lasting impression that he had lost everything. Losing everything leaves one with nothing, making one worthless. Jesus was not emphasizing this state of being in the younger son, as debauchery and recklessness are common trappings found in a material world.

From this identification, it is worthwhile to see how this son is like the last of the three servants of the master, as established by Jesus in another of his parables, the one commonly called the Parable of the Talents (or Minas). It was to the third servant that his master gave one talent (wealth), only to find later that the servant buried that treasure in the earth. That burial was also a wasted talent, which compares to this son's wasteful actions. Like the third servant, this son had been given a divine purpose in life; but rather than use that God-given gift to bring others away from their slumbers in a world of pleasures and delights, the younger son did nothing to bring out his spirituality as the voice of the Father. Therefore, it can be assumed the younger son, like the third servant, heard God (the Master) say (in his

Parables Explained: The Parable of the Prodigal Son

mind), "I tell you that to everyone who has, more will be given, but as for the one who has nothing, even what they have will be taken away." (Luke 19:26, NIV)

The Greek words written, "*zōn asōtōs*," state an addition to not using his talents of purpose, such that he was "living prodigally." It is important to realize that the Greek text has those two words separated from the others surrounding them by comma marks. This separation makes "living prodigially" be important to fully grasp.

The word "prodigal" means, "wastefully extravagant" and "having or giving something on a lavish scale." The Greek word "*asōtōs*" means, "extravagantly wasteful because of 'loose living,' i.e. a debauched, profligate lifestyle." (HELPS Word-studies) The word that is missed in this separation is "living," where "*zōn*" is rooted in "*zaó*," meaning, "I live, I am alive" (Strong's) and "I experience God's gift of life." (HELPS Word-studies) This says the son born of God into a human form was not having a purposeful effect on the world, not "living" up to his potential. Instead, the world was effecting the son negatively, to a great degree.

In this regard, let me flash an image before your eyes before continuing on with my analysis of this reading. It is easier to see a "prodigal son" as frivolously experiencing life, than it is to see the world wasting the son's wealth of talent. In this regard, get the image is of a televangelist that plays to the heartstrings of a viewing audience, knowing the world is messed up and there are many people desiring someone to confirm what they know spiritually, as in explaining the words of the Holy Bible to them. By telling the people what they want to hear, the televangelist is not fulfilling a purposeful life predetermined by God. He or she is burying a talent to attract listeners; but equally important are those who want to hear, extravagantly wasting their talents to seek the truth, only to be easily misled. One is prodigal for personal gain: mansions, jet planes, jewelry and fine clothes, etc. The other is prodigal by a dependence on other human beings, having lost all faith in God.

Now that the image of a truly prodigal son has been cast, look at what happens in the story next. Famine strikes the world.

After the son of the Father had mingled with those of the world, as one of the world and not one of God, all the talent that was his inheritance from the Father had been squandered. In lush times, when plenty abounds, no one wanted to hear someone say, "Repent! A better world awaits in heaven!" No one would listen, only saying in return, "Look around you brother. Is this not heaven on earth?" It takes a famine to bring one to one's knees in repentance.

The Greek word "*limos*" translates as "famine," but equally means "hunger." The word suggests a scarcity of food; but in this parable told by Jesus, the pervasive "hunger" is not about physical nourishment . The word's use is meant to point to a spiritual need that is absent. The world has fallen into a state where the Word of God cannot nourish the hearts and souls of mankind.

The verse that has the translation "there was a severe famine in that whole country," this is like the prior verse that said the son "set off for a distant country." Here the repeated Greek word "*chōran*," from the root "*chóra*," should be realized as being a statement about the physical world. The impression given of a "distant country," which was then suffering from famine, makes it seem easy to justify the son eventually returning home to the father's estate. However, the word "*chóra*" means "land, as opposed to the sea." (Strong's "B") The deeper meaning is then that the "earth, as opposed to heaven" was in great need of spiritual food.

From that perspective, the statement that continues, "and he began to be in need," shows how the body of the son of God had become lost. He was realizing his shortcomings, which were based on the "share of the estate" given to him by the Father. The buried talent was then buried too deep to quickly recover.

In verse fifteen, where the translation above says, "So he went and hired himself out to a citizen of that country," the story paints a clear picture of a destitute son, who has become the servant of another, as a "hired hand." From that translation, one must grasp the lowering of self this symbolizes, having come from God's "country" (the spiritual realm or heaven), so the son has found need to serve a human being. However, the Greek word "*ekollēthē*" (a form of the root verb "*kollaó*") means more than going out and finding a job or someone to work for.

The word "*kollaó*" comes from "*kólla*," meaning "glue." It then means, "to bond (cleave), adhere to (literally, "glued together"); to cleave, join to; (figuratively) intimately connected in a soul-knit friendship." (HELPS Word-studies) The son found a "bond" with another "fellow citizen" (from the Greek "*polités*"), which says he married someone who also had a talent to serve God, becoming a mentor to the younger son. By "cleaving" to another who was devoted to God, the Holy Spirit reached out and touched the younger son.

When you now read the story, see the spirit of the son as having entered a world of plenty, which was wildly lavish in its self-indulgence. The talent that was the son was wasted in a world that was too self-involved to receive the purpose of spiritual life. However, once the world reached a saturation point and was glutted with excess, it could no longer enjoy the excess of plenty and began to hunger for more. It was this hunger in the younger son that led him to find a partner that was not blinded by what all the world has to offer. This is the lesson that money does not buy one love.

This means the son was not "hired" as a worker, but became one with another human form of flesh. The word "*ekollēthē*" is only found written in this verse fifteen of Luke 15. Still, the same root word produces "*kollēthēsetai*," in Matthew 19:5, which states, "For this reason a man will leave his father and mother and be united to his wife, and the two will become one flesh.' There, Jesus was quoting Genesis 2:24.

The point that must be gained from this word's use in the parable of the prodigal son is that the son, due to hunger for spiritual purpose to be fulfilled, became united with "a citizen of that country," or "a fellow citizen of the world." Notice how those references also tell of a son leaving his father, for the purpose of cleaving, two into one. Two is then a number that is closely associated with the Apostles and their evangelism, where they went into the world in pairs, being representative of the need for support offered by a Church (souls together as one in Christ, not buildings).

Parables Explained: The Parable of the Prodigal Son

With that union understood, see how the "famine" was not so much a physical presence in the world, as the son was "sent to the fields to feed pigs." Returning to the use of the word "*chóra*" as meaning "country," the word also strongly implies "fields," in the plurl. Here the Greek word written is "*agrous*," which also means "fields," but also "a country estate." (Strong's usage) Thus, the younger son, once fortified by companionship that enables his purpose and talent to surface, returns to the world to sow and reap as God intended him to do.

Questions that should arise at this point, if the son was starving for food are: How could he hold "feed" in his hands and not eat? If a "citizen" owned "pigs," are they not raised with the objective being to slaughter them and eat their flesh? If the son's gift had totally been wasted, what would keep him from further debauchery and stealing the pig's feed or killing the pigs? The answers gained from these questions help one see the younger son had changed spiritually.

We then read, "He longed to fill his stomach with the pods that the pigs were eating, but no one gave him anything." This gives the impression that the son had become addicted to the ways of the world; but the symbolism is missed by thinking the son wished for pig slop.

The Greek word that has been translated as "stomach" is "*koilian*." The root word ("*koilia*") actually means, "belly, abdomen, heart, a general term covering any organ in the abdomen, e.g. stomach, womb; met: the inner man." (Strong's) While the word "stomach" or "belly" fits in a parable story of fiction, the symbolism that has to be grasped is "inner man" or "innermost being." (NASB

Translation)

According to Thayer's Greek Lexicon (#5 usage), the word imitates the Hebrew word "בֶּטֶן," or "*beten*," so its usage implies "the innermost part of a man, the soul, heart." The Hebrew means "womb, abdomen," as where one "conceives to bear children." Therefore, the son was not hungry for pig slop. Instead, he desired someone to feed his purpose in the world, which was a fertile place to plant the seeds of the Father.

By seeing this, one can then look at why Jesus said the son was delivering the "the pods that the pigs were eating."

The Greek word translated as "pods" is "*keratiōn*," which is specifically a "carob pod." The word literally means "a little horn," due to the shape of the fruit of the carob tree. Thayer's Greek Lexicon states: "the name of the fruit of the κερατέα or κερατεια (or κερατια), the Ceratonia sillqua (Linn.) or carob tree (called also St. John's Bread (from the notion that its pods, which resemble those of the 'locust', constituted the food of the Baptist). This fruit is shaped like a horn and has a sweet taste; it was (and is) used not only in fattening swine, but as an article of food by the lower classes: Luke 15:16."

Because the last definition (of food for the lower classes) references the appearance in this parable, that assumption should be disregarded as Jesus was not speaking in metaphor to make the listeners think carob pods were pig slop. The point about the locusts of John the Baptist is more important to grasp.

That usage of definition makes it possible now to see that

the "famine" was self-caused, making it representative of self-sacrifice, like the forty days Jesus spent in the wilderness. The "carob pods" or "locusts" that John the Baptizer lived on in the wilderness represent the spiritual food that the innermost part of a man (or woman) needs, before one can begin to serve God completely. The "pods," also termed "little horns," must be seen as the morsels of the Torah (spiritual food) that the Jews fed on routinely. The fact that the "pigs" became fat from eating those "husks" from the carob tree says they profited from the poverty of spiritual nourishment that the Jews were fed.

This drought of spiritual sustenance made going to the "swine" of the world, where "*choiroi*" ("swine" or "pigs") is synonymous with Jesus saying, "Give not that which is holy unto dogs, nor cast your pearls before swine, lest they trample them underfoot and turn to rend you." (Matthew 7:6) The same metaphor does not literally mean a four-legged animal, but acts as a reference to one who is gluttonous, or excessively greedy.

The use of "pigs" would be how Jesus saw the dangers of the world that existed in the ruling class of Jerusalem, to whom Jesus was telling the three parables found in Luke 15. They were those referenced when Jesus continued by saying, "no one gave him anything." The younger son gave of his spiritual insight about the "pods" those "pigs" loved to eat, but Instead of them giving thanks in return, they turned on the son and tried to destroy him.

We next read, "When he came to his senses," but that is again a misleading translation. The Greek states (literally), "the point reached or entered of purpose himself now having come." This means the preaching ("feeding pods to pigs") had an effect on him, even though no one else cared about what the son was saying. It was not because of intelligence that understanding came to the son, but from the inheritance given to him by the Father. He stopped trying to be like all the others and started being what he was meant to be. At that point, the son opened his mouth to speak and the Holy Spirit came flowing out. His ears were hearing Scripture explained in ways none of the "pigs" had ever taught, and those explanations were coming from his lips.

That is the purpose of one Greek word set off by comma marks: "*ephē*." That word means more than simply, "he said," but speaks of the son's realization of his purpose, as "he was saying, declaring, and/or bringing light by asserting one statement over another." (Strong's and HELPS Word-studies)

This is when we hear Jesus speak the dialogue of the son, not so much as a confession of his shortcomings for having not realized his purpose sooner, but as what he heard himself telling those who gave him no favorable response in return. The son said:

"How many of my father's hired servants have food to spare, and here I am starving to death! I will set out and go back to my father and say to him: Father, I have sinned against heaven and against you. I am no longer worthy to be called your son; make me like one of your hired servants."

This translation, of course, is not what was truly written by Luke, relative to what Jesus told the Pharisees and scribes who had complained about the company Jesus kept. The first sentence asks (in two segments), "How many hired servants of the father of mine have an abundance of bread , I however with hunger here am perishing [dying]?"

The substitution of "food" for "bread," when carob pods were a physical form of "food," enough to fatten pigs so pigs could be slaughtered for "food," overlooks the metaphor of "bread." According to HELPS Word-studies, the Greek word "*ártos*" (or "*artōn*") means, "properly, bread; (figuratively) divine provision; all the sustenance God supplies to yielded believers scene-by-scene to live in His preferred-will." As Jews, who professed to be superior to Gentiles due to the Laws of Moses and them being descended from the children of Israel, they had an "abundance of divine provision," but they were "perishing" by not being able to satisfy their "hunger" that was caused by an inability to understand that which had been provided by the Father.

The son spoke those words to the Jews, but only he understood the meaning. This means "How many of my father's hired servants have food to spare, and here I am starving to death" is akin to the lament of the *Ancient Mariner*: "Water, water everywhere, Nor any drop to drink." For all the Scripture the Jews had at their disposal, and for all the handling of the scrolls they did routinely, very little was satisfying the needs of their souls.

Next, our ears hear the son saying, "I will set out and go back to my father and say to him." What is importantly missing from this translation is the first word of verse eighteen, which is (like "*ephē*" before) set off by comma marks, making it an important one-word statement.

That Greek word is "*anastas*," which translates as "having

risen up." The importance of this one word goes well beyond the simplicity of standing from a crouching or sitting position, to mean an "elevation" of Spirit, where Strong's adds the root word ("*anistémi*") means "I rise from among (the) dead" and Thayer's Greek Lexicon ("**I c**") says the word implies "to cause to be born." That reflects back to the "belly" or "stomach," where the word "*koilian*" stated a desire to be filled in the "womb if the inner man." We are misled by not reflecting on an elevation of Spirit taking place as the son spoke.

The statement is then separated into two parts, where the translation simply shows this with the presence of the conjunction "and." The word "and" is the Greek word "*kai*," which has 9079 occurrences in the New Testament verses. To read a simple conjunction as the meaning is to say that God speaks in redundant, meaningless words. In the English language a comma is a mark of punctuation that implies "and," making the writing of "and" superfluous and unnecessary. In the Greek written by Luke in verse 18 there is a comma, followed by the word "*kai*."

From my work in understanding the French of Nostradamus, the symbol "*&*" was written many times, without him ever writing the word "*et*." That symbol's usage signals it acts as a marker of importance, not simply a redundant statement of more. This means a mark (symbol or word) that says "and" or "in addition" is less important as a word of conjunction, becoming a great notation of what to focus close attention on next. As such, "*kai*" is written to draw close attention to what is stated after, as an important addition.

This means the son, "having risen" in Spirit, said, "I will

go to the father of me , **and** I will call him". This has to be seen as separate statements of the son's having become elevated in Spirit, where the "will" of the son has been replaced within his innermost being by the Will of God. In the future first person indicative voice, Jesus was then stating what "will" occur to the son, where "will" is based on the direction of the being from then on. Therefore, the son "will go to the father," who "will become of me," and the voice of the son "will call" from having become one with "him."

Relative to the two verbs that state the "will" of the future of the son, the first written is "*poreusomai*," which has been translated as "I will go." According to Strong's, the usage of this word states, "I travel, journey, go, die." This last option of translation ("I die") is the key one to focus upon.

According to Thayer's Greek Lexicon (b), the word "*poreuo* " is: "By a Hebraism, metaphorically, α. to depart from life." This then leads to the site adding, "β. to follow one, i. e. become his adherent." From this, one has to hold in one's hands of understanding and get the feel that the son has "to depart" or "die" of self-ego, in order to relinquish all the trappings of a mortal world, where there is nothing being given in return for faith in God. From sacrificing oneself to the Will of the Father, one then "will go to the father of me," where "of me" ("*mou*") is a statement of self, "of I" ("*egó*"). Once that death (departure) has taken place, then ("*kai*") "the call" made by the "*egó*" will be "him."

Rather than a colon mark, as shown in the NIV above, the statement, "I will call to him" is followed by a comma, with the one word "*Pater*" standing alone, another comma following it. This is a statement, via capitalization, that the one ("him") called forth is God Almighty, the "Father." The capitalization takes this beyond a simple "man who has two sons," making it known the son is a soul from God. This means the son has died of self ("I will depart") and subsequently is able to speak for the Father, as the Father alone (stand-alone word). This, again, is just as Jesus said, "I am in the Father as the Father is in me."

Now, what is read next appears to be the son planning out in his mind how he will go back home and address his father, admitting he has been defeated by the world. However, that should not be read into what the "Father" will have made come from His son's mouth. What the son is "called" to say, at the "Father's" command, is:

"I have sinned against the one heaven *kai* before you."

Notice the presence of *kai* splitting this statement into two parts, with "before you" ("*enōpion sou*") implying "before the face of you," being introduced as important to grasp.

The Greek word "*enōpion*" (from "*enópios*") means, "before the face of, in the presence of, in the eyes of" (Strong's). HELPS Word-studies adds: "*enōpion* – literally, "in the eye (of God)," used for how all things happen under God's watch, i.e. in keeping with His plan built on His absolute knowledge."

Knowing that meaning adds greater power in this statement by the son, more than as if he confessed, "You saw all my sins." It adds importantly (the *kai*) that the eye of God has allowed the son to see all of his sins that have turned him "against the one heaven," which relates to that purpose of life God intended his son to live up to. Confession is then more than words to return to a purpose, but the act of repentance that backs up the words.

When this is seen as a voice inspired by God speaking through the son, it becomes possible to better understand the follow-up statement, which the NIV translates as, "I am no longer worthy to be called your son." The literal Greek translates to state: "no longer I am worthy to be called son of you" (from "*ouketi eimi axios klēthēnai huios sou*"). This is an amphibological statement that is confusing by design, as the same words can be read in opposite ways.

To grasp this best, it is important to see how the Greek word "*eimi*" is a statement of "being," and how the Greek word "*klēthēnai*" (as in the aorist passive infinitive tense) is a verb set in the future sense of "being," as "to be called" or "to be named." For this to be clearly seen, then the statement's words "*ouketi eimi*" should be read as a preliminary statement that says, "no longer am I," which is then a clear statement of "not being" self-ego driven. It is then that change of "being" that makes the son "worthy to be named [God's] son" ("*axios klēthēnai huios sou*"). The son's mouth can voice those words because he has submitted his self-ego to the Will of the Father. Thus, because he is "no longer **I**" he is "worthy to be called the Son of God."

Following a semi-colon (in the Greek and in the translation above) the inner voice of the son states, "make me like one of your hired servants." This has to be viewed in the context of the parable's story, where the son has made himself the "hired servant" of someone in the distant land that is suffering from famine and is given nothing but the carob pods to slop pigs with (and they are not for him!). This leads one to see the son imagining how much better life would be if he could go back home and live on his father's farm as one of the workers. This, however, ignores that the voice of God is speaking through the son, who has surrendered his self-ego to serve the Father completely.

The first word in this new statement, the Greek word "*poiēson*" (translated into English above as "make") is a word that bears two intents, with both viable through the voice of God. The first meaning becomes a statement of the son being made, manufactured and/or constructed by the Father, where the purpose is what makes the son worthy. It is why God made the son originally. The second meaning becomes a statement of the son being caused, done, and enacted by God's Will, not the self-ego of the human flesh. Thus, the first word of this statement by the younger son ("*poiēson*") places focus on what works must be done by the son that are the qualifications for worthiness.

The next key word to examine is "*misthiōn*," which is translated above as "hired servants." The singular number of this word in Greek means, "a paid worker, hired servant, hireling (contrasted with a slave)," where a "servant" is not someone forced into subservience, but one who willingly submits to a role of service with some form of payment in return. The voice of God eliciting thoughts from the son is then stating the realization that God the Father made the son to be a willing servant, knowing there would be a fair reward in return for services rendered.

With that seen, the next thing to discern is the transformation from "me" (Greek "*me*," a form of "*egó*") to "of you" (Greek "*sou*"), where "like one" is stating the singularity of God the Father, not the son. The Greek word "*hōs*" is translated into English as "like," but fully means, "as, like as, even as, when, since, as long as," with usage directing one to understand "about, as it were, according as, how, when, while, as soon as, so that." (Strong's) This adverb is not the son saying that he knew he would remain a special "one," but treated as equal "as" the "servants." Instead, it says the Father is leading the son to realize that all "servants" are those who become "one" with the Father, giving up the "me" of them to become the "you" of God.

By grasping the completeness of depth found in this conversation in the son's mind with the Father, we see that the word stating "having risen up" ("*anastas*") is repeated. Repetition is an important element in the divine Word, which means that a repetive being omitted following the question (stated by the NIV as an exclamation [!]) "How many of the servants of my Father's" misleads the serious reader. The repetition, most simply understood, eliminates it as a physical statement of getting up from a lowered position, as nothing is stated that repositions the son in a lowered physical stance.

The word "*anastas*" confirms the spiritual elevation the son's soul has achieved, with the sacrifice of self-ego, so he can further rise in Spirit to enter heaven in his soul state. The importance here is introduced by a capitalized "*Kai.*" That states the great importance of the son "having risen up" (a powerful one-word statement even without the *Kai*) marking reading guidance), so he could "go to the father of himself."

We then have translated into English for us, "But while he was still a long way off, his father saw him and was filled with compassion for him; he ran to his son, threw his arms around him and kissed him." The Greek text states: *"eti de autou makran apechontos , eiden auton ho patēr autou , **kai** esplanchnisthē , **kai** dramōn , epepesen epi ton trachēlon autou **kai** katephilēsen auton ."* Notice the differences in the punctuation from the translation into English (NIV) and the Greek. A literal translation restates this as: "still now he far being distant , saw him the father of him , and was moved with compassion , and having made progress , fell upon the neck of him and kissed him ."

This becomes a series of six segments that make separate statements of importance, with two powerful one-word statements introduced by the word "*kai*." The fifth and sixth segments are divided by the word "*kai*," making the last two words ("kissed him") require separate analysis, while knowing this is a statement conjoined with an embrace ("on the neck").

The sequence states:

• The son has not reached heaven, as he is still alive in the world ("being distant," where the word "*apechó*" truly means, "to have one thing by separating from (letting go of) another" (HELPS Word-studies) in his risen state of being.

• The son is elevated to the state of seeing through the eyes of the Father, such that the Father is in the son as the son is in the Father.

• The son is moved by compassion that comes from the Father. This is important ("*kai*") as the emotions of the Father are strongly felt within the son.

Parables Explained: The Parable of the Prodigal Son

- Next is an important statement of the urgency this strong emotion within conveys, as the word "*trechó*" conveys an athletic desire to "run," as an "intense desire to get to the goal as quickly as possible." (HELPS Word-studies) There is the insight of progress having been made that warrants this urgency. As such, the Father is quick to be with the son with the rush that is the onset of the Holy Spirit.

- The words that state "upon the neck" are then a statement of the head that is separated from the body by the neck, with the neck offering the flexibility to change fields of view. The progress made is then within the mind of the son.

- The words that state "kissed him" are then importantly ("*kai*") stating the love and affection that the Father coming within the son brings.

This says that the son was in flesh and bones as a servant to God the Father and it was that commitment to God that was "seen" by the Father "from afar," such that the embrace that "ran" to the son was the Holy Spirit. While the metaphor of a parable makes it sound like the flesh and blood father of a long lost son kept him on the lookout for his son's return, the symbolism has to match the reality of Jesus and the lessons he was teaching to his disciples.

To tell this story to the blind and deaf Pharisees and scribes, they heard it the way priests and laypeople hear the story read aloud in churches today. It is most important to grasp the deeper meaning, because the parable is the third of three told about something lost being found. The son is no different than one sheep in a flock of one hundred, and no different than one silver coin out of ten. This must be understood in order to grasp how the son is one of two sons.

When the story then states, according to the NIV English translation above, "The son said to him, 'Father, I have sinned against heaven and against you. I am no longer worthy to be called your son,'" this appears to be the son reciting what he had practiced before, when he was lost and without food. The Greek text actually begins with the capitalized word "*Eipen*," which places importance in the word "Said." The lower case spelling of the word means "He spoke, said, told, or conversed. The third person gives the impression that "he" is the son, but the capitalization infers that the voice is God's coming through the son's lips.

When the quote that is attributed to the son (not the Father through the son) begins with "Father," it is natural to assume the son is speaking to someone who has just come and hugged him, showering him with kisses. The Greek separates the capitalized word "*Pater*" with commas, meaning this is a powerful one-word statement about who is speaking. The deeper meaning then becomes God knowing the inner thoughts of the son, so when the son does speak it is the "Father" knowing all about the son's prior confession. This is important to grasp as it explains why the Father ignored what the son supposedly said and it explains why the son would not make such a confession (in reality) if his father had just run down a country road and greeted him with open arms and warm kisses.

It is important to see the part of the mental thought that states, "I am no longer worthy to be called your son" as being in the first person. The Greek word "*hēmarton*" states "**I** have done wrong," or "**I** have been lost," or "**I** have missed the point," or "**I** have made a mistake." It is the self-ego of the son that is recognized as the root cause of the "sin against heaven."

The introduction of "*kai*" then places important separate focus on "I" being the lower-g god that was "against" the Father, because the son's ego became a god "before" the true God. That is an admission that the son broke the First Commandment, where the Greek word "*enópios*" means, "before the face of, in the presence of, or in the eyes of." (Strong's) As long as "I" exists as an all-important being of Self, Self will always come first, making one always act as a god, before the Lord is recognized as God. It emphasizes the greater sin is from seeing Self as an equal to God, more than one succumbing to worldly allures (as all humans do).

With God the Father then with the son via the Holy Spirit, knowing the heart and mind of the son has truly repented for his sin of Self-will, the only response that should be expected is forgiveness, which means a celebration of redemption. This is the reason the next verses state: "But the father said to his servants, 'Quick! Bring the best robe and put it on him. Put a ring on his finger and sandals on his feet. Bring the fattened calf and kill it. Let's have a feast and celebrate."

Again, the actual Greek begins with the capitalized word "*Eipen*," restating the importance of the Father's voice being the source of the son's thoughts in conversation – Spiritually. The missed double entendre that comes from the NIV English translation comes when "the father said to his servants" is read as meaning the "servants of the father," where "him" (or "his") is ambiguous.

In reality, the Greek word "*doulous*" does not translate as "servants," as "*misthiōn*" does (meaning "hired servants"). Instead, it translates as "slaves" or those "enslaved." Further, the word "*pater*" is not capitalized, such that it no longer refers to God the Father.

This means the statement "Said" by God is to the son, who had become the "father of slaves," which were the worldly addictions to sin the son had been lost among. It is to those "slaves" (or demons within the son's fleshy brain) that God then commanded: bring out the robe and good clothes; give him a ring for his hand; and place sandals on his feet. Following a semi-colon and the word "*kai*," the fatted calf was brought out, killed, and eaten, bringing out a joyful celebration.

That sequence of events makes a clear visual in a parable, but the metaphor speaks loudly as the son having become a priest of the Lord (the best robe) and he had been clothed in righteousness, with all the drapings of sin removed [forgiveness]. The ring then symbolizes the soul of the son being forever married to the Father, where the rings symbolizes eternity (from a circle) and the hand makes the son the hand of God on earth. Us humans place rings on our left hand finger, because the left hand is closest to the heart; but the lack of distinction as to which hand is placed the ring, "hand" (from the Greek word ("*cheira*") means, "the instrument a person uses to accomplish their purpose (intention, plan)." (HELPS Word-studies) The son's purpose was to find his way back to heaven and eternal bliss (the ring).

The sandals placed on the feet are symbolic of heavenly powers given by the Holy Spirit that keep the lowest part of human flesh (the feet, which Jesus washed the feet of his

Parables Explained: The Parable of the Prodigal Son

disciples in the last Passover Seder) from ever again getting the filth of worldly sin upon the son. From being able to walk among evil without it influencing the son, the fat of the land is killed and burnt as an offering to Yahweh. This makes the son a high priest, just as was Jesus in the Christ, so the element of eating becomes a feast of spiritual food that forever is the need of a high priest.

This abundance is then the value of marriage to God the Father, as his bride, regardless of one's human gender. Males and females are expected to marry God in order to become His priests and truly Christians, reborn as Jesus His Son.

With these verses understood, the "prodigal son" ceases being the focus of attention and the shift is placed on the "elder son." This is where the element of two brings up the lessons of the Old Testament and the repetition of multiple sons born to the "elders" of Israel. First, there is Cain (the elder) and Abel, born to Adam and Eve. Second, there is Ishmael (the elder) and Isaac, born to Abraham and Hagar-Sarah. Then, there is Esau (the elder) and Jacob, born to Isaac and Rebekah. The repetition says that the elder is always the one who expects everything to come to him by birth, but does nothing to secure that.

The "prodigal son" of this parable is like Abel, in that he was a shepherd (he "kept flocks"), who was a priest that sacrificed the lives of his animals to please God. He is like Isaac in his willingness to sacrifice himself (to death), if it pleased God. He is like Jacob in his understanding the error of his ways and returning to seek forgiveness and lower himself before the brother he wronged.

This makes the elder son become a reflection of the anger

in Cain, the jealousy of Ishmael, and the threat of Esau. As two from the same Father, the "younger son" now becomes a reflection of Jesus and the "elder son" becomes a reflection of the Temple of Jerusalem – the religion of Judaism. The "elder son" will soon be shown to be the true wasteful one, making him be the true reason this parable is known by the title "prodigal son."

Jesus was telling this parable to those who made the claim to be God's "elder son," as those who cast blame on Jesus for eating with tax collectors and sinners. This parable is now driving home the point of their unreasonable rejection of Jesus as the Son of God. In the same way that Cain let sin overwhelm him, finding delight in revenge, and never becoming repentant, so too would the Temple of Jerusalem rulers complain before God about one who won favor, while they had been denied.

The Greek word that established the son of the end of the story as the "elder" is "*presbyteros*." That word means "elder," but also conveys this meaning: "A member of the Sanhedrin, an elder of a Christian assembly." (Strong's) It is "properly, a mature man having seasoned judgment (experience); an elder." (HELPS Word-studies) When scholars jump at the presence of "inheritance" at the beginning of this parable, pondering how the religious scholars who were listening to Jesus must have been aghast at a second son expecting his inheritance early, before his father's death, surely they would have heard "*presbyteros*" and thought, "Is he talking about us now?"

The same scholars do not ever consider how Jesus was telling this parable (told through the Saint that was Luke) to us (especially the religious scholars), so the same word means

Parables Explained: The Parable of the Prodigal Son

Jesus mocked "mature men of seasoned judgment" who are "of a Christian assembly." The same moral of this story fits the scenario then, of a Temple of head-strong men who rejected the Son of God as a "wasteful son," to the scenario now, of Churches that make the "prodigal son" one son only, just as the "elder" is only one son (not the many each son represents).

Notice how the elder son "was in the field, (from the Greek "*agrō*"), which is the same place Cain toiled. The Greek can translate as "a field, especially as bearing a crop," but equally can be a statement of "the country, lands, property in land, a country estate." This repetition is overlooked as the same worldly place where the "younger son" roamed with his "share of the estate." It says both sons had been set out into the world with a purpose as their inheritance.

Still, "the field" was the realm of Cain. The symbolism of the altars built by Cain and Abel can now be seen as the fruits of their labors being sacrificed to please God. Abel sacrificed an air-breathing sheep to the Lord and it pleased Him. Cain, on the other hand, sacrificed the fruits of the earth, which had no breath in them. God was not pleased by Cain's labors that served the world-earth mother-material plane, as burning them simply returned them to a material state, from a material state (ashes to ashes, dust to dust). Abel released the spirit of a living sacrificial animal to God and burned the flesh so the spirit rose with the aroma of fire and smoke.

In that same way (remembering that God was not pleased with burning vegetables), the "elder son" was not approaching the Father from an experience that sacrificed his soul to serve God. He was simply living off the wealth of the Father, doing little to earn his respect (the lack of any rewards for staying on the "farm"). Thus, the "elder" son was angry that the Father celebrated a son that had been worldly but sacrificed that to return to God.

When the translation states of the elder son, "When he came near the house, he heard music and dancing," this obliterates the punctuation of what was actually written (thus actually said by Jesus). The series of word segments begins with the word "*kai*," stating the importance that needs to be grasped by the elder son "like as coming" (from "*kai hōs erchomenos*"). Whereas the elder son had been working in the fields, he too was "coming" to the Father's house, just as had the "younger son" returned there. This use of the present participle "coming" must be grasped singularly as the purpose of religion, which the "elder" reflects. That role is to lead others to God, so they can enter into His heavenly house.

The next segment of words states, "he drew near to the house," where the focus established by the separation with commas is the "elder son" (symbolizing the churches of Christianity, the synagogues of Judaism, and the mosques of Islam) is to go to heaven. All roads from the "fields" lead to that end.

The next segment of words in this series then is a double statement (containing a non-separated by commas "*kai*"), which says, "he heard music **and** chorus." The Greek word "*chorōn*" typically translates as "dancing," but the word "*symphōnias*" (the harmony of musical instruments, "symphony") is better paired ("and") with the sound of a "chorus," rather than the loud feet stomps of dancing.

Parables Explained: The Parable of the Prodigal Son

The implication of the importance of the one word "*symphōnias*" is "dancing" implies joyfulness and emotional outlet through the vibrations of music. However, when heaven is realized to be the "house," then the "chorus" should be realized as the heavenly angels that constantly sing praised to God. This is the powerful statement made by the sounds of heaven that resonate to the faithful of earth, as heaven sings out the promise of a soul being rewarded for devotion to God.

The English translation above then has the elder son call upon one of the "servants" (from the Greek "*paidōn*"), which should be read as a heavenly angel of the Lord. The Greek word "*proskalesamenos*" says the elder son "having called near," meaning he summoned this servant to give him answers. This is a statement that the elder son feels godlike in his relationship to the Father, making him equally capable to call upon the ethereal entities to serve him, when they are in fact the "slaves" of the Father, not the sons. This becomes the self-righteous state of religions, which associates their devotion to God as an equal authority to act as gods on earth.

When we read that the elder son asked the servant, "what [is] going on"? the question says the elder son has never done anything to enter the "house" of the Father. This is a reflection of how the institutions of religions that are dedicated to the One God do not have any experience of what heaven truly is or what joy and happiness goes on there. That is a statement against them ever having been filled with the Holy Spirit.

The sounds of music and chorus that praise God loudly and sweetly are not like anything heard "in the fields." The "music **and** symphony" is the vibrational excitement of one's soul in the flesh, with the Christ Mind letting the flesh experience heaven on earth. The elder son has not ever known the Christ Mind.

The "servant" then responds with the truth of the situation, where the younger son has returned "safe and sound," causing the Father to sacrifice worldly delights (the young bull [the one] fattened [by the grains of good fruit]) in honor of that. The Greek word "*hygiainonta*" is actually written, which translates as "in good health" or "pure, uncorrupted." (Strong's) This animal sacrifice should again take one back to Abel, whose animal sacrifice pleased God, unlike that of Cain, who burned the fruits of "the fields."

The next verse begins with the capitalized Greek word "*Ōrgisthē*," where the capitalization shows a greater power coming from the statement, "Angered," "Irritated," or "Provoked." The capitalization is then a statement of the rage that filled Cain when God had recognized his brother's sacrifice, but not his. This is then a powerful statement of the elder son's urge to kill, simply because he (or it) was not recognized for all the works (done in the fields) he had accomplished. HELPS Word-studies adds to the lower-case meaning of this word: "*orgízō* ("to show settled-opposition") is positive when inspired by God – and always negative when arising from the flesh. "Sinful (unnecessary) anger" focuses on punishing the offender rather than the moral content of the offense."

This says the elder son was enraged, just as was Cain. This is confirmed when we then read, "[the angered elder son] refused to go in." This is a rejection of heaven, just as Cain rejected God and lay on the ground letting evil thoughts fill his brain. Likewise, when Cain lay on the ground angered, God came to him, speaking to Cain: "Why are you angry? Why is your face downcast? If you do what is right, will you not be accepted? But if you do not do what is right, sin is crouching at your door; it desires to have you, but you must rule over it." (Genesis 4:6-7, NIV) In this parable, Jesus has the Father also come to address a tantrum, appearing to beg ("pleaded with him") the elder son to listen to reason.

The Greek words that are actually written that tell of God the Father begging His elder son are: "*ho de patēr autou , exelthōn , parekalei autou*". The English words translated by the NIV above show no breaks or commas, showing, "So his father went out and pleaded with him."

These three word segments state a progression of events that parallel the story in Genesis 4, of God coming to Cain. The words written can allow the first segment to state "case next father the same (self)," which is a statement of God being one with the elder son, so the two can communicate. Prior to this, the elder son had sought out a "servant-slave" of his Father. This progresses that to the elder son and God being together, just as God had "run" to be with the younger son.

This leads to a one-word statement that becomes powerful and important because it is set apart by commas. The Greek word "*exelthōn* " that can both mean "having gone out" or "having come out." Stemming from the root verb "*exerchomai*," this word reflects back on the use of "*erchomenos*," where the elder son was shown to be "coming" from the fields. It says that the anger of the elder son, like the anger in Cain that drove him to have his "face downcast," became a plea to God from anguish in the elder son's heart, driving him to his knees calling upon the Father.

When this progression is clearly understood, then the final word segment that relates to "begging" is not the Father seeing His elder son throwing a tantrum and pleading with him to be reasonable, but the son "pleading" to the Father, for Him to do things for that benefit him. The word written, "*parekalei*," better translates as "sending for, summoning, and admonishing," with one limited use being "begging." This is a statement of selfishness in the elder son, just as the selfishness that made Cain angry in his heart for the lack of favor shown him by God. It was from that lowered state that those parallel sons called upon the Lord.

With this twist seen, the following Greek word "*apokritheis*" (which is translated into English by the NIV above as "answered") is actually the present participle "answering," but better conveys, "taking up the conversation." (from Strong's usage) Rather than the elder son knowing his Father has come "to respond" to his selfish pleas, the elder son continues his argument against finding out his brother has been welcomed into the house of the Lord, with a burnt offering of fatted calf, while his labors in the fields has left him without God's favor. Therefore, the conversation continues, as the details of the elder son's calling upon God.

This is where the translation above has the elder son crying out, "Look! All these years I've been slaving for you and never disobeyed your orders. Yet you never gave me even a young goat so I could celebrate with my friends." The boasting about what "**I** have" done and what has not been done for "me" is pure selfishness, blinded from seeing why he toils in the fields. Rather than tend living creatures, it was the elder son that decided to do the opposite of the younger son and not pastor flocks. This is then seen in the elder son mentioning that he thought it was God's responsibility to reward his dedication to worldly works with an occasional "young goat," which can be offered up in celebration to God, with the elder son and his Temple-Church-Mosque friends feeling exonerated for their works on the material plane. These claims by the elder son are most revealing.

First, it is the elder son who uses the capitalized Greek word "*Idou*," which is a statement that God the Father needs to "Behold!" or "Look!" or "See!" worldly accomplishments as the elder son sees them. This one-word statement, separated by comma marks, is a statement of the elder son taking the stance of being equal to God. This one word powerfully announces the godlike image of himself, as if he had been given the right to pretend to be a god on earth. There is nothing God the Father does not "Behold!" as He is omniscient.

Second, the elder son says (literal translation from the Greek), "so many years I serve you," where the Greek word "*douleuó*" means, "I am a slave, am subject to, obey, am devoted," again being in the first person of "**I**." This is a statement of years of service demanding some recognition.

This is the same argument Cain had with God, because God did not show him favor for his sacrifice of vegetables, even though Cain labored more in the tilling of the ground and the reaping of a harvest, while his brother simply opened a gate to a pen and whistled as the sun was setting, letting the flock do all the work. This becomes a parallel to all who feel their devotion to their (possessive pronoun) god or God by some name is based on longevity of belief, not the results of their works serving that God. This is the blindness of selfishness that makes one desire to make God work for one, not one understanding his or her need to work for God. As self-perceived gods, by saying "**I** am a slave, **I** am subject to, **I** obey, or **I** am devoted," they are projecting unto God His equal commitment to be their slave, subject, obedient deity, or devotee to the time served (which is only possible in a linear world that has the illusion of time).

Third, the elder son says, "**I** never disobeyed your orders," where the Greek word "*entolēn*" is better translated as "commandments" or "laws." Knowing that Jesus is telling this parable to the Pharisees and scribes who were obviously wealthy from their positions as godlike men of robes and all authority based on knowledge of the Laws of Moses (they were "lawyers"), the elder son is crying out his anger for being like the rich young man who asked Jesus, "How can I be assured of going to heaven [going into the Father's house]?" The first thing Jesus told him was, "Of course, you know there is the laws," at which point he listed some The young rich leader (an "elder" or "*presbyteros*") made the same claim as does this fabricated character, saying, "All these things I have kept from my youth," which boasts of length of service to "the laws" of God. To obey the Law, it always helps to actually know what the laws mean; but being selfish has the problem of making oneself make up the meaning, rather than submitting to God the Father for His insight. That is, in itself, disobedience.

From that selfish anger comes next, "Yet you never gave me even a young goat so I could celebrate with my friends." The Greek of this statement begins with the word

Parables Explained: The Parable of the Prodigal Son

"*kai*," rather than "yet," meaning it is important to grasp the two central aims of this series of words: "young goat" ("*eriphon*") and "friends" ("*philōn*"), which are the central foci of a two actual statements split by a comma mark.

The Greek word "*eriphon*" means "young goat" or "a kid he-goat," but HELPS Word-studies adds this: "(figuratively) any person not submissive to Christ, especially the unredeemed who are rebellious against God to the core." When this lack of submission to Christ is considered, relative to Jesus using this word symbolically before Pharisees and Temple scribes, the parallels to Jesus telling his disciples about the sheep and goats, the parable of the Good Samaritan told as a point of rejection to Gentiles, especially those who were formerly Israelites, and the Temple's regular practice of animal sacrifice, says the "young goat" represents the lack of proper sacrifice by themselves, just as Cain had not been given an animal to sacrifice to win God's favor. As metaphor for the descendants of God's chosen people, such that a "young goat" would be representative of Isaac being an offering for Abraham to sacrifice on the altar, none of the remnant of Judah had been made capable of winning back their land, with a "young goat" becoming a new King David. All of this lament is then for what 'would-coulda-shoulda' come to be, but was never given to the re-creators of Jerusalem by God, despite all their years of service to a lost contract.

To add to this complaint ("*kai*"), it was important to see that their 'land' or seat of power (Jerusalem, in Judea and Galilee) was still owned and controlled by Rome and its governors. The lament about not having that gift so "that I might make merry with my friends" (translation that is closer to the actual Greek) was the age old demand of the wayward Israelites, made to Samuel, when they demanded that he should give them a king. They demands "then we will be like all the other nations, with a king to lead us and to go out before us and fight our battles." (1 Samuel 8:20) The "friends" are the recognition the Temple-Church-Mosque believes the world owes it, for simply being there as a powerful entity that cannot be destroyed by bad kings, because God (by whatever name) loves them so much. That concept is a selfish mindset that loves to celebrate in its divinity, without ever doing anything divine. The selfishness prevents that; and Israel and Judah were overcome by bad kings because of their lack of divine submission and a disregard of self.

The elder son then goes on to say (according to the NIV English translation), "But when this son of yours who has squandered your property with prostitutes comes home, you kill the fattened calf for him!" This translation is misleading and not actually what is said. The literal Greek translates into four segments of words, with one a one-word statement set off with two commas. The translation based on the word order in which it was written states, "at which time now the son of you this , the [one] having squandered [or devoured] your all living among prostitutes [or an idolatrous community] , came , you for him have killed the fatted calf !"

As should be seen as different between the two translations is the Greek text says nothing about "possessions" having been squandered. In fact, the Greek text, "*ho kataphagōn sou ton bion meta pornōn*," is so ambiguous that "*ton*" is not typically translated, as it is an article usually meaning "the," the same as the lead word "*ho*." This means the language should literally state, "the having devoured you [or your] the living with [or among, or of place] prostitutes [or an idolatrous community]!" I have offered above a viable translation, which is based on the same ambiguous words having been acceptably translated elsewhere in Scripture "the [one]" and "all." Seeing this ambiguity cleared in this manner, while also knowing the new story being told by Jesus, says the elder son is pointing out the younger son as having wasted the gift given by the Father, which is not "possessions" but purpose.

The son calling the world a place of idolatry, where "living" is a soul in a human body, rather than squandering things, is the pot calling the kettle black. The elder son is just as guilty of having come from the fields of Temple-worship, where the standard method of operation is to call sinners out, as the Pharisees and scribes had done at the beginning this whole series of parables. It was they who were "living with prostitutes," because they sold themselves for profit and gain every day. This is why there was no animal sacrifice in their honor (just as Cain found no favor from God) because the fields had been their "fatted calf." They chose material gains over heavenly rewards. The same plight exists today, in all forms of religions calling YHWH their God (by different names).

From this exclamation of distress, similar to that of Cain after he did not gain God's favor, the NIV English translation says God responded. We read, "'My son,' the father said, 'you are always with me, and everything I have is yours." Unfortunately, this too is misleading, as it incorrectly has God calling the elder his "son."

The literal Greek leads up that address, where "*Ho de eipen auto*" leads to a comma mark, which can be translated to state first, "All [or That] on top of this [or next] answered [or commanded] him." This has to be read as the response by God the Father, but the capitalization of "*O*" ("*Ho*") makes this first word important to grasp.

As "All," which was the translation before when the elder son was complaining about the younger son's wastefulness, having squandered "all," that collective (as "That" previously referred to) is now used by God to identify the elder. The importance of "All" is now the history of the elder son in the fields, which is the entire lineage of the ones who claim to be the children of God. Therefore, "That" or "All" is the point of the "answer" to "him."

Next, the comma at the end of that segment of transition words, from the elder speaking to the Father answering, is one word set apart by a following comma. That word is "*Teknon*," which is also capitalized, showing an important address being made. That Greek word does not mean "son" but instead means "a child (of either sex)" [Strong's definition] or "a descendant or an inhabitant." [Strong's usage]. HELPS Word-studies adds, "(figuratively) anyone living in full dependence on the heavenly Father, i.e. fully (willingly) relying upon the Lord in glad submission. This prompts God to transform them into His likeness."

When "All" is seen as a reference to lineage, then "Descendant" is an identification of the elder being one of the Tribes of Israel, upon which the Covenant created a dependency on the Father for their land and wellbeing – a Covenant that was broken repeatedly, with "All" land lost. It is most important to see the Father calling the elder by a term that is less "son" and more "Child [of God]."

Parables Explained: The Parable of the Prodigal Son

After that address, instead of the translation stating, "you are always with me," the better translation states, "you ever after mine are." In this more literal translation the element of time is not "always," but "after a starting time," which is then a statement of when Moses came down with the Covenant. The Greek words "*pantote met'*" needs more focus placed on the use of "*meta*," where it is not a simple preposition stating "with," but (according to Strong's usage) "(2) after, of time, with nouns, neut. of adjectives."

The reference can then be seen as the Father (God) speaking to all who were "Children" (from "*Teknon*") of Abraham, Isaac, and Jacob (Israel), with the promise of "always" being those chosen by Yahweh. The time began "after" ("*met'*") the people told Moses, "We will do everything the Lord has commanded. We will obey." (Exodus 34:7, NIV) It was "after" that commitment that they were "forever" bound by their ancestor's pledge. The elder son was thus a "Descendant" in that line of committed Israelites.

The Father then continued His response to the "Child" of Israel, with the next two segments of words being set off by comma mark and the first segment beginning with the word marking importance, "*kai*." The commas bring new light to what has been translated as "**and** everything I have is yours." The literal Greek now translates as two statements: "***kai*** all that mine , yours to be".

In this breaking into two statements, the Greek word "*ta*" (the nominative neuter plural article "the") is reference to the "always after" as "that," or as the pronoun "they" or "them." The possessive word "*ema*," as "(is) mine," says the Covenant is God's, not from the demands of the people.

As such, "ever after" is relative to the eternity of the Father and His determination of who has proved their commitment to His Covenant … "mine." With that grasped, the second segment of words says that God will determine who is "mine," based on the actions of the people, relative to God's Covenant. God made the demands that establish who is His "Children," and that is then is up to the people "to be."

Seeing this response, knowing the metaphor is God as "the Father," makes it clear that God is not an appeaser of bad acts, as the elder son had just demonstrated. He threw a tantrum akin to Cain's and God did not run to tell His crybaby "Child," (in a coddling voice) "There, there. Everything is okay. Look at all I have given you." Instead, the Father is slapping the moral of this story onto the elder, by saying, "If you want what your brother received, then you know what is expected of you as well." Those demands were set for eternity when Moses came down the mountain with the Covenant.

In further response, the Father then explained that "to celebrate and be glad" was the proper response that should be given the returning son who had wandered, because he had fulfilled the letter of the Law as it was intended to be observed. The translation above (NIV) then explains this as being "because this brother of yours was dead and is alive again." In reality, the Greek text also splits this into three segments of words, which better describe the situation.

The literal Greek translates to English as: "because the brother of you this , dead was , *kai* he lives." This says that both sons were given the same Covenant to follow ("*houtos*" as "this"). In both cases, where the elder was given an eternal soul within a body of flesh, the same as the younger son, they were "brothers" as "members of the same religious community" (which is relative to both Jewish and Christian descendants today). Still, a soul in a body of flesh reflects the death of mortality in that state of being. By being allowed to serve God the Father as human beings, they both "were dead" in that state. Being "dead" can only be changed through adherence to the Covenant, which is the same for both brothers that are "Children" of God. However, in the younger son's" case, importantly ("*kai*") "he is alive" or "he lives." The reason for making merry and rejoicing (from "*euphranthēnai*" and "*charēnai*") is due to the "dead" son having gained eternal bliss in heaven … something the elder son had not earned and did not deserve.

This then leads to the moral of this longer parable to be the same as the two shorter parables told first: "he was lost and is found." Still, this NIV translation misses the separation of those two states of being. The Greek text states this literally as, "**kai** he was lost" (from "*apolōlōs*") "**kai** he is found." The use of "*kai*" makes both states important to grasp.

It applies to all human beings born into the flesh as "he, she, it is lost" in a material state of being. Each has the same value of purpose that is each's own to discover and live up to. That discovery comes through the Gospel that brings with it knowledge of the Law; but living up to the Law cannot be done alone. Both sons were equally lost in different ways. Both were sought, but only the one who received the Holy Spirit "was found."

This is why Jesus told these parables to the scribes and

Pharisees, who stood in the same Cain-like, "elder son" position of expectation of inheritance, without having to do anything to find the truth of the Word. Everyone is then born as a wasteful "child" of God, in possession of a soul, which means God possesses the body of flesh … all are His. God sends His Son to find the ones who want to be found. That is why Jesus dined with tax collectors and prostitutes, because they all wanted to be found by God. The scribes and Pharisees, however, refused to listen to Jesus.

Parables Explained: The Parable of the Prodigal Son

The Parable of the Rich Man and Lazarus

Luke 16:19-31

FOREWORD: This is a rather long explanation of a well-known Biblical story. It is a rather simple (seeming to be) story of a repeated lesson that warns the wealthy believers in Yahweh, while giving solace to the poor of faith. It is so seemingly simple to grasp that it is easy to 'ho-hum' it and just yawn. I was led to look at it deeper than I had before and was surprised to see what is sweetly hidden in the verbiage that makes this lesson told by Jesus take on a fresh appearance.

Recently, my writing on a book had me researching the mythology behind the names of the planets. What I learned about Pluto was very interesting, which is most befitting the discovery of that orb (since downgraded to a dwarf planet or planetoid). Pluto was discovered in 1930, with the element plutonium discovered in 1934, and produced and isolated in 1940, named as an honor to the discovery of a new planet. Pluto became symbolic of the dawning of the nuclear age. The same Greek word from which "Pluto" comes is the same word from which comes "rich man" in this reading (and others of similar focus).

One important thing I found in this reading is relative to

each of the characters being named, when it appears only Lazarus stands out. The name Lazarus is representative of a class of people, making the "rich man" also be representative of the same. Therefore, we are all today either one or the other. As such, I write this in-depth explanation for all who might want to know this. Still, it is less for the Christians that sit in pews and more for the ones who will stand before the pewples. My hope is they will give this lesson the proper attention it deserves.

> "There was a rich man who was dressed in purple and fine linen and lived in luxury every day. At his gate was laid a beggar named Lazarus, covered with sores and longing to eat what fell from the rich man's table. Even the dogs came and licked his sores.
> "The time came when the beggar died and the angels carried him to Abraham's side. The rich man also died and was buried. In Hades, where he was in torment, he looked up and saw Abraham far away, with Lazarus by his side. So he called to him, 'Father Abraham, have pity on me and send Lazarus to dip the tip of his finger in water and cool my tongue, because I am in agony in this fire.'
> "But Abraham replied, 'Son, remember that in your lifetime you received your good things, while Lazarus received bad things, but now he is comforted here and you are in agony. And besides all this, between us and you a great chasm has been set in place, so that those who want to go from here to you cannot, nor can anyone cross over from there to us.'
> "He answered, 'Then I beg you, father, send Laza-

rus to my family, for I have five brothers. Let him
warn them, so that they will not also come to this
place of torment.'
"Abraham replied, 'They have Moses and the
Prophets; let them listen to them.'
"'No, father Abraham,' he said, 'but if someone
from the dead goes to them, they will repent.'
"He said to him, 'If they do not listen to Moses
and the Prophets, they will not be convinced even
if someone rises from the dead.'" Luke 16:19-31,
NIV

The Greek text of this lesson taught by Jesus, recounted
by Mother Mary to the doctor Luke, begins with a statement about each of two men. Both are identified as "certain," from the Greek word "*tis*." This identifies each man
as known individually, while identifying two who were
associated with many like them. Their "certainty" is what
bonds two of opposite status levels together in this story.
As a lesson taught by Jesus to the Jews of Galilee, that
use of "certain" then spoke of specific members from their
religious group. Therefore, the two men identified in verses
nineteen and twenty were not people of uncertain religious
beliefs, as each adhered to the principles of Mosaic Law.
Being Jewish was "certain" of both men.

The second man is identified as "certain," with this further
specified as "named Lazarus," from the Greek words "*ono-
mati Lazaros*." The mistake that is made in reading those
two words that way comes from thinking one man was
named Lazarus, which eliminates other symbolic meaning.
That not only ignores the meaning behind the name, but it
disconnects all later students from relating to the characters
true **Christ**ians are supposed to be seeking, to be reborn

as Jesus Christ. When one reading this lesson realizes that Jesus spoke in metaphor about Christians today (those who are supposed to be "in the name of Jesus Christ"), then understanding the meaning behind that name "Lazarus" is most important.

The name "Lazarus" (Greek spelling "*Lazaros*") is "the Hellenized version of the Hebrew name רזעלא, *Eleazar*." (Abarim Publications) The name is then like "*El-azarus*." The Hebrew meaning of the root name is then "God Has Helped" or "Helped Of God." (same Abarim Publications source)

The capitalization should then not be read as simply stating a proper name (a syntactical rule of the English language of this story. Reading that there was a "man named Lazarus" into a teaching by Jesus leads all who read these words or hear them read aloud in a church and think, "Well this is about somebody long ago 'named Lazarus' who I have no affinity with." The mistake comes from not seeing oneself as "Lazarus."

The truth that Jesus spoke to a Jewish audience bears deep meaning to all Christians also. Christians are supposed to be founded in the principles of Mosaic Law ... at least those commonly termed "the Ten Commandments" ... but that misleads, taking one away from the importance of the meaning behind a name), but a significantly important word of meaning, which identifies more than one human being. "Lazarus" is intended to be one character of parable that reflects upon a whole class of faithful that are like "Lazarus."

This means the capitalized word "*Lazaros*" is making two statements. First, it is stating the importance of the One

God (*El*) in all who believe in Yahweh. Second, it is stating the importance of all who are "named" as "certain," being relative to a specific religious set of beliefs commanded by *El*. That name is then a statement of all who see the value of the Laws of God, through Moses, as worthy of complete commitment and submission. Therefore, "Lazarus" is not naming one person but naming all Jews and Christians who "God Has Helped."

When one has become comfortable overcoming that limitation of the word "*Lazaros*" and understands how the capitalization makes this lesson be pointed at every Jew and Christian who believes in Yahweh, the question should be, "Then why is Lazarus (one who God Has Helped) identified in the translation as a "beggar"?

It is important to read these verses (or have them read aloud in one's presence) and question, "I feel like I have been helped by God, because I am a successful person; so why is one Helped Of God laid at a gate as a beggar?"

One needs to ponder, "If I am truly helped by the One God, how am I reflective of one who is covered in sores?"

The reasoning should be to find out who oneself identifies with in this teaching, as Jesus was not only speaking to a group of Jews in Galilee when he gave this lesson. The reasoning should be to see Jesus speaking to everyone who will read his words forevermore. The reasoning should be to understand what one has overlooked in the past, as a student called again to listen to a lesson with a more mature mind.

First of all, verse twenty begins by stating the Greek word

"*ptōchos*," a word that is not capitalized. English syntax calls for the first word in a sentence be capitalized, but Biblical Greek text is following divine syntactical rules. The word "*ptōchos*" translates as "poor, destitute, spiritually poor, either in a good sense (humble devout persons) or bad." (Strong's) The lack of capitalization says (silently) that poverty is not an important issue. The lack of material wealth is not an issue for any whom God Has Helped. As this story (eventually) tells of "Lazarus" going to Heaven, one should assume the identification is to one who is "a humble devout person," whose "poor" status does not deter God from having his needs met, as a devoted servant. The result of one "Helped Of God" is one is "poor" due to a lack of material needs.

HELPS Word-studies states, relative to Jesus' usage of "*ptōchos*," the word's usage acts as an assumption of a reduction in physical stature, which leaves one a beggar. They state: "*ptōxós* (from *ptōssō*, [meaning] "to crouch or cower like a beggar") – properly [means], bent over; (figuratively) deeply destitute, completely lacking resources (earthly wealth) – i.e. helpless as a beggar. (*ptōxós*) relates to "the pauper rather than the mere peasant, the extreme opposite of the rich.""

This word's usage has led translators to paraphrase what Jesus said, making his words be twisted, creating a misleading visual by saying Lazarus "was laid a beggar." In reality, those who belong to the class of people "God Has Helped" are "bent over" to Yahweh, subservient to His Will. They are "lacking earthly wealth" that simply keeps them from identifying with the materially "rich." IF there are any sores visible on their bodies, the sores signify the admission of their sins, which places them prostrate before the gate of Heaven, begging for forgiveness from God.

In the most basic sense, every child of God (especially those seeking to be true **Christ**ians) must see him or herself as pitiful without God's help. As a part of every confession of sin, there should be an earnest plea for God to forgive and assist in the acts that will eliminate further sins. In this regard, all ones of true faith are beggars before the Lord. To receive God's help, one must first help God, which requires begging for the strength to do the work of God alone.

Knowing this about the identification of one "God Has Helped" makes not seeing Lazarus as a beggar easier to fathom. The descriptive term that makes this lesson of Jesus more powerful says that the person identified as Lazarus was the "extreme opposite of [one who was deemed] rich." [HELPS Word-studies] Seeing a lame beggar covered in sores as helpless, reduced to seeking crumbs [metaphor for alms for the poor] for survival, makes it quite difficult to grasp the evil of a "rich man." It almost excuses being rich today, while caring little about how many poor people there are in the world, as if with the attitude, "They should pray to God more."

Understanding that verse twenty is Jesus setting up a lesson where the one "Helped Of God" is the "extreme opposite of the rich" means looking closer at verse nineteen is important. The literal translation of that verse states, "A man now certain existed rich , **and** he was clothed in purple and fine linen , making good cheer every day in splendor."

This verse has three segments of words, set off by the presence of comma marks. It is important not to erase this punctuation (whether it is imagined or real), as it keeps one from paraphrasing what was written. Paraphrase is a trick of human language, but it is the application of syntax not spoken by Jesus.

In addition, I have found that wherever the Greek word "*kai*" (typically translated as "and") appears it should be read as a statement of importance to come (that which is stated next), rather than as simply stating "and." English syntax frowns on placing "and" and a comma mark together; so when we see ", **and**" above, this concept that "*kai*" is written-spoken as a mark of importance to come is supported. Strong's Concordance states that "*kai*" is written in the New Testament 9079 times. That repetition should be viewed as more significant than simply being a stuttering use of "and," like "oh yeah, add this."

The comma mark separates like a conjunctive word ("and"), while the word "*kai*" acts as a signal of importance to follow. This non-translation of "*kai*" as a conjunction (which finds many are deleted from translation, due to redundancy) also means that where it is written "purple **and** fine linen" there are two statements made. By simply stating "and" (the trick of syntax again), the mind quickly computes "fine purple linen," missing the importance of "purple." The word translated as "fine linen" is a separately important description that follows the symbolism of the word translated as "purple." The word "*kai*" says, "See the separate elements, "purple" followed by "fine linen."

When one read verse twenty previously and found that "certain" was followed by "named Lazarus," where "*Lazaros*" was less about the name of a specific person but an identification of all devout believers in the One God (and all to come), the parallel should be seen in verse nineteen. There, the word "certain" is followed by the Greek word *"plousios,"* which has been translated as "rich man." This should be seen as a parallel 'name', just as is "Lazarus." The word *"plousios"* is defined as meaning, "rich, abounding in, wealthy; subst: a rich man." (Strong's) This says that the translation as "rich man" is a substitute for the true meaning. Realizing that means *"plousios"* is how this "certain man" is 'named', which separates him from all uncertain wealthy people, misses that he, like "*Lazaros*," is named "*Plousios*," without the importance of capitalization.

HELPS Word-studies adds to this understanding of usage as such: "*ploúsios* (an adjective, derived from 4149 /*ploútos*, "abundance") – properly, fully resourced; rich (filled), by having God's "muchness" – i.e. His abundance that comes from receiving His provisions (material and spiritual riches) through faith (4102 /*pístis*)." This is another way that seemingly justifies seeing value in the "rich man," as his wealth is assumed to be due to his "faith." That assumption allows one to wrongfully think, "rich duds on the outside correlates to a wealth of inner goodness."

This later assumption of "God's muchness," which includes "material riches," must be seen as not fitting the set-up that is opposite the lack of material concerns sought by one "God Has Helped." Yahweh, as the One God, does not help His believers become materially "rich," making this lesson demand seeing that truth. Despite the mega-churches that have 'slick Willy' preachers in thousand dollar suits that only preach, "Jesus wants you to be rich," that is a lie that does not match what this lesson by Jesus teaches.

It is better to remember what Jesus said to his disciples

later in his ministry. Then he said, "Truly I tell you, it is hard for someone who is rich ["*plousios*"] to enter the kingdom of heaven. Again I tell you, it is easier for a camel to go through the eye of a needle than for someone who is rich ['*plousion*'] to enter the kingdom of God." (Matthew 19:23-24)

Jesus said that after he told a young man [one who owned lots of possessions and was a ruler of the Jews (Pharisee)] how to be assured of going to heaven. The young man walked away sadly, after being told that following the Law was (of course) required, but the key to getting to heaven was this: "If you want to be perfect, go, sell your possessions **and** ["*kai*"] give to the poor ["*ptōchois*"] , **and** [", *kai*] you will have treasure in heaven. Then ["*kai*" translated as a capitalized "Then"] come, follow me." (Matthew 19:21)

It becomes important to see how the "certain man" of verse nineteen is then given the name of "*plusious*" (lower-case of insignificance), just as the "certain man" of verse twenty was "named Lazarus." The lack of capitalization is then a statement of the lack of importance that Jesus gave to all believers who (exactly like the rich men of Jerusalem and Galilee when he taught) place wealth as a statement of their piety. This makes the substitute translation of "rich man" realize another substitute implication, as an identifying name - both for an individual and a group of Jews [and Christians].

The Romans named their god of the underworld Pluto, because Pluto was a form of "*plusious*." Pluto's etymology, according to the Wikipedia article "*Pluto (mythology)*" is: "*Plūtō* (genitive *Plūtōnis*) is the Latinized form of the

Greek *Plouton*. Pluto's Roman equivalent is *Dis Pater*, whose name is most often taken to mean "Rich Father" and is perhaps a direct translation of *Plouton*." The Romans revered that lesser god as the god of abundance (and with abundance comes power and influence). The equivalent Greek god was named *Hades*, who was not revered in any way by the Greeks. However, the Romans saw the underworld as from where the riches of the world came, as mineral rich ores that were mined from under the earth's surface.

By seeing this in verse nineteen, Jesus gave the rich man the extreme opposite name to "God Has Helped," as being one specifically who the god of the underworld has helped. Conversely, one who worships a god of underground riches can be viewed as being name "One Who Has Helped Oneself." Verse nineteen can be read as naming an individual Jew named Pluto (or *Shepha* or *Mamónas*), but only if there is just one man named Lazarus. The two men must be seen as metaphor for two groups of human beings, representative of those Jews and Christians who are just like one of those two men. Both claim to be believers in Yahweh; but the verse nineteen group (*"plousios "*) pays homage to two masters, while those of the second group in verse twenty (*"Lazaros "*) begs of One God.

This awareness means that it was abundance that enabled the "certain man" of verse nineteen to be "clothed with purple." The Greek word *"porphyran"* is a color that represents "power or wealth." (Strong's) Purple is the color of the robes of kings, because they wield the power and wealth of nations of people, whose "certainty" is a nationality more than religious beliefs. To wear that color was then a statement of royal status. More importantly, it was a Self-assumed state of power and influence, as no Jews in Galilee or Judea were truly of royalty.

At the time that Jesus taught this lesson, the "certain" Jews of Jerusalem had the power and wealth of the Second Temple that allowed them to pretend to be royalty. The fall of Israel and Judah was due to their ancestors having followed their human kings to ruin. The were no kings in Jerusalem after Herod the Great died, and Herod owed his royal dynasty to his Roman masters that placed him in power and supported his reign. The Roman Emperor(s) sought to pacify the Jews of Jerusalem by letting them think they ran a city state within the province of Judea; but after Herod died that region was placed under a governor from Rome. After their return from exile in Babylon, the ruling class Jews of the Herod's Temple had forgotten that God should be their King.

This means the use of "*enedidysketo porphyrin*" ("he was clothed in purple") is a statement that one who claimed to be a Jew (today a Christian or believer in Jesus Christ) was "putting on airs." He (and all like him) "was clothed in" the invisible robes of Self-importance, based solely on how much wealth one had amassed (at the expense of others). The extreme opposite view that fits this segment of words is "putting on the clothes of righteousness." Righteous is not the view one should have, when reading what Jesus said identifying the one as "rich" ("*pluto*").

Evidence in this regard comes from the Apocalypse of John, who wrote of righteous clothing in two verses. He wrote, "But you have a few people in Sardis who have not soiled their garments; and they will walk with me in white [not purple], for they are worthy." (Revelations 3:4) John also wrote, "It was given to her to clothe herself in fine linen, bright and clean; for the fine linen is [metaphor for] the righteous acts of the saints." (Revelations 19:8)

Support is also found in the books of the Old Testament. Isaiah wrote of righteous clothing: "Righteousness will be his belt " (Isaiah 11:5); "righteousness as his breastplate" (59:17); "in a robe of his righteousness" (61:10); and in a negative sense of failing to serve God, "all our righteous acts are like filthy rags" (64:6). Zechariah 3:4 also spoke of this, writing: "The angel said to those who were standing before him, "Take off his filthy clothes." Then he said to Joshua, "See, I have taken away your sin, and I will put fine garments on you." Further, David wrote, "Let your priests be clothed with righteousness, And let your godly ones sing for joy" (Psalm 132:9).

All of this becomes statements of the opposites of physically being "clothed in purple" and the spirituality of wearing "clothes of righteousness." By understanding the words of the prophets, one is capable of seeing how those of "certain" faith, who served in the Tabernacle, were serving for material rewards. Those priests who would wear the sacred garments of the servants of Yahweh appeared in "filthy rage," not the garments of kings.

The use of "*kai*" says that simply dying common clothing the color "purple" was not all the ones of abundant wealth did. They enhanced that signal of royalty greatly by adding that color to "fine linen," which could have been "purple" or any other color when purchased. The Greek word used by Jesus is "*bysson*," which [according to HELPS Wordstudies] means, "fine linen, i.e. a very expensive (sought-after) form of linen – "a specific species of Egyptian flax or linen made from it that is very costly, delicate." (J. Thayer)."

This means that in addition to putting on the clothes of self-glorification, rather than the clothes of righteousness, the people who were like this "certain man" always made sure people could tell their status by the clothes they wore, knowing their fabric was imported. This is like men and women today that wear expensive suits that clearly say, "I am powerful." It reflects an inner drive that forces one to selfishly live up to the English saying: "You have to spend money to make money." More money must be reinvested in self-appearances and airs.

The comma then leads to the final segment of words that add detail to this acting like royalty that separates oneself from the common class of people by dressing in finery, all because one is of a "certain" faith. The Greek states "*euphrainomenos kath' hēmeran lamprōs*," which literally translates as "making good cheer every day in splendor." This says, basically, the abundance of one's position of wealth has made them "feast" ("*euphrainomenos* ") twenty-four-seven ("*kath' hēmeran*") on the finest of everything ("*lamprōs*").

This makes the sum of verse nineteen be about one's opulence, which is a sign of one's decadence caused by wealth. That means: If Yahweh has initially given one abundance, then it was as a test of faith. Jesus told the young rich Pharisee how to pass that test and be "perfect." However, that young ruler walked away sad, reflecting how most rich Jews (and Christians today) fail to deal with "abundance" properly (much less perfectly). The projection of self-worth, while ignoring the "poor," is an imperfect state of being that keeps one from heaven.

When one has a firm grasp of verse nineteen being about everyone of Judaic-Christian values (who believe in Jesus Christ's lessons), it points to those who misjudge wealth as God's blessing for them to rule the world. When one can see how "*Lazaros*" is a powerful statement of true Christians that have been filled with God's Holy Spirit and been reborn as Jesus Christ (bearing his name as "God Has Helped"), then it is easy to see how verse twenty needs some translation adjustments, so that those who are the extreme opposites of the rich are not seen as crippled beggars.

Verse twenty's Greek states two segments, separated by one comma mark: "*ebeblēto pros ton pylōna autos , heilkōmenos*." That can literally say about "God Has Helped" ("*Lazaros*") that one of His faithful "was thrown to outsiders porch same , being full of sores." This is because "*ebeblēto*" (from the root "*ballō*") means, "to throw, cast," in a stronger sense than "laid" implies. The translation of "laid" gives the impression (somewhat) "with care" or "gently." The Greek word "*pylōna*" refers to "a large gate; a gateway, porch, vestibule," meaning something more significant than a private gate to a country villa on a dirt road. It implies an entrance to a palace, which fits the royal motif of "purple" robes and "fine linen."

It then is a statement that this "certain poor man" of Jewish faith was denied access to the inner courts, deemed too poor to gather along with well-to-do Jews; or "thrown" outside the Temple proper, to the Court of the Gentiles, which was beyond the Beautiful Gate and near Solomon's Porch.

Following the separation from a comma mark, the Greek

word "*heilkōmenos*" states the one exception to this general banishment. If one was "covered in sores," then one could gain access to the Court of Lepers, in the general area of the Women's Court, not far from the Nicanor Gate. Still, it would be better to stand outside the temple with "outsiders," even if the rich and powerful saw that association with Gentiles as sores covering one's body.

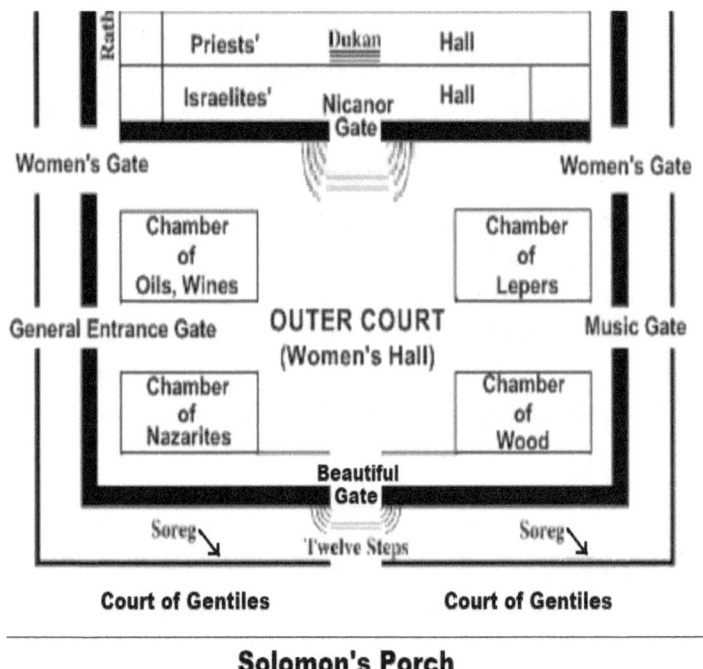

The Greek word "*ton*" simply translates as "the," but NASB (New American Standard Bible) lists three times it translates as "outsiders," and four times as "others." The implication is then creating the imagery of one being "cast" When "*pylōna*," is realized to translate as "a large gate; a gateway, porch, vestibule," then this word should be seen as representing Herod's Temple - a fixture of Jerusalem.

The words *"ebeblēto pros ton pylōna"* then paint the picture: "Cast towards (the) others' gate to them."

When verse twenty-one begins by stating *"kai,"* this is again signaling a level of importance that is relative to "longing." The Greek word *"epithymōn"* means "desiring," usually in a negative sense of lustful wanting or longing; but it also means "setting one's heart on," where the heart is the seat of the soul. As one named "God Has Helped," one can make the assumption can be made, in this case, that the soul of Lazarus (his heart-center) was pure. Therefore, "to be fed" (from *"chortasthēnai"*) is less a reference to physical food, and more a statement of needing one's heart be fed with spiritual food. Lazarus represented one (of many) who went to the Temple "to be fed" the nourishment of God's Word.

The Greek word *"chortasthēnai"* bears the meaning, "to be satisfied, filled," where there is an emptiness that needs filling or satisfaction; but that does not necessarily mean in one's belly. To desire such nourishment that is "to fall from the table of the rich man" makes this a statement of lack from the "rich man," rather than plenty that is shared. Since no one places a "table" (*"trapezēs"*) in one's 'driveway', by a "gate," Lazarus was never able to see the "table" of the wealthy. That Greek word, when associated with money, implies a "money-changing or business" "table," from which Lazarus was denied. However, the strong implication becomes the golden Table for the Showbread that was on the north side of the Sanctuary.

The commandment of God was, "**And** you shall place showbread on the table before Me at all times" (Ex. 25:30) Every Shabbat twelve new loaves of bread, prepared in specific pans, would be set on the shelves of this table, with the old loaves removed. The miracle of this exercise was the twelve being removed (a week old) were said to be just as hot and fresh as when left there. It was Sanctuary priests who performed this duty saw this as a Divine Blessing by God. The old loaves (presumably) were then the bounty of the priests (as was the choice cuts from the animal sacrifices), such that consuming Divinely Blessed bread would cause them to be also inspired by God. Those priests, along with the scribes, Pharisees and Sadducees, would then be expected to be influenced by God to give blessing to the masses. One like Lazarus could expect no more than a "crumb" of this goodness.

This means that those who pretend to be holy (based on abundance of wealth) and wear fancy clothes that include priestly robes rarely (if ever) produce morsels of insight that nourish the souls of the faithful. Still, the sequence of words actually states (from the Greek), "from that falling from the table away from the table of the rich man," where the Greek word "*piptontōn*" equally states, "falling under (as under condemnation)" and "falling prostrate." This is then not waiting for food to fall from a dinner table, but "falling down" from having been outcast ("falling under" the decrees of royal priests) and praying to God ("falling prostrate") outside the Temple gate. It makes the reference to "falling" be prayers for guidance from God.

The translation that has verse twenty-one concluding with the statement, "Even the dogs came and licked his sores," needs refining. The new sentence is confusing, as the word for "dogs" ("*kynes*") implies "scavenging canines," who ran wild and were disdained by the citizens. For Lazarus to be portrayed as a lame beggar that was hungry for crumbs to keep him alive, one would assume a stray dog would likewise compete with him for any crumbs. To lick his wounds, after stealing his crumbs, would be like adding insult to injury. However, this segment of words is poorly translated.

Following a semi-colon mark (absent in the translation above) is the word of exception "*alla*." That means "but" or "however," such that there is a caveat being stated by Jesus, one that is relative to this "falling from the table of the wealthy." After notice of an exception comes the Greek word "*kai*" again, which prepares one for an important statement to follow. That statement comes in three segments, which literally can say: "but **kai** outsiders dogs , coming , were licking clean this wounds the same."

The exception is then pointing to the importance of "*ta kynes*," or "the dogs." It is the presence of "*kai*" that alerts the reader to look for meaning that is greater than a simple article (a, an, or the). In this regard, the word "*ta*" is another that typically translates as "the," but the NASB lists the same translation options as "outsiders" or "others" (seen prior for the Greek word "*ton*"). This way of seeing that translation working here, where "*ta*" is identified as important, means that "outsiders" become the Gentiles that were also barred from the tables inside the Temple. This makes "dogs," the literal translation of "*kynes*," refer to the figurative translation of the word, so "dogs" is a statement (importantly) of the way the elite Jews viewed Gentiles.

The one-word statement next, between two comma marks, is "coming." This is then relative to those who were not Jews, but came to the Temple just to stand outside. This would have been Samaritans and Greeks, or any of the scattered Israelites who had become mixed blood, while still believing in the God of their ancestors who were Israelites. It would be outside the Temple that teachers (like Jesus, and later his Apostles) would offer insight about Scripture. The Gentiles came for those morsels falling from the table, rather than hoping to get inside where nothing of importance was ever said. Thus, being among those who were seeking to find God, whether Jew or Gentile, all "were licking the wound" of banishment, exile, and rejection for past sins unforgiven. That is especially true for those of great faith, as not being able to join with those of "the same" stated religious beliefs (the "certain") is hurtful.

The aspect of "covered in sores" and dogs licking "sores" is what makes it seem that some man named Lazarus was a leper and a poor beggar (perhaps lame too). In the times of Jesus, people like that would have been banned from holy spaces and blamed for their physical plights. "Sores" were seen as outward projections of imperfections stemming from one's inner being, which were then deemed as evidence of sins.

The Greek root word "*helkos*" means "a wound, a sore, an ulcer," often used to denote a "(festering) sore." (Strong's) Still, the one-word statement that assumes one person was "full of sores" can also allow for the assumption that one was treated like a leper, when the only 'sores' that covered his body were from the honest wear and tear a poor man of values earns from hard labors.

When invisible "sores" are angers that fester within one's soul, due to unfair treatment at the hands of the rich and powerful (with no recourse other than suck it up and bear it), there is no doubt a faithful follower of Yahweh would be falling prostrate before God asking for forgiveness and strength to continue. This becomes reminiscent of Job.

Job was an upright man who suffered mightily from sores he did not deserve. Job fell prostrate before the Lord, as he blamed himself for not knowing what sins he did to bring about his plight. Never was Job found blaming God for his plight (although others advised him to do so).

It is very important to see this lesson of Jesus from the perspective of two (individuals and groups) who have been placed on God's scales of judgment. God would judge both men (just as God judges all human beings), based on each individual's faith as "certain men" who claimed to serve Yahweh. They would not be judged by how much wealth and abundance one had or who had physical maladies that others saw as evidence of sins. God's judgment is based on souls that have no flesh to drape with finery and no flesh to ooze from sores.

This becomes quite evident after both have died. God's judgment found the one who professed faith in Him (a "certain man"), but lived only to satisfy himself and deny others, as being worthy of entering an eternity of suffering. The one who served God (a "certain man") and was identified as "God Has Helped" ("*Lazaros*") was "carried away by the angels" and taken to the embrace of Abraham in the spiritual realm. The one who most pew-sitting Christians today would root for (as many see themselves in that man), would be the one to go to a burning place.

This is where one must understand that Jesus was not teaching about two imaginary individual characters. He was speaking instead with metaphor, of all who were identified as Jews, which has evolved today to the present state where it includes all who identify as Christians (including Jews). Jesus told of the fate of everyone who claims to be devoted to Yahweh. His lesson says: Be rewarded in the material world by the joy of fleeting riches, and know the soul will suffer in the afterlife; or, be assured that the soul will be rewarded in the spiritual world by eternal bliss, after momentary suffering in a world that is careless.

This lesson is no different than when Jesus said, "No one can serve two masters. Either you will hate the one and love the other, or you will be devoted to the one and despise the other. You cannot serve both God and money." (Matthew 6:24) The word for "money" is "*mamónas*," which many have translated as the personified deity Mammon. The lower case can make that statement, as Mammon was a lesser god, not close to earning the distinction of personification where capitalization states important. Still, so many worship "money" as their god, when that "love of money" means a hatred of Yahweh (regardless of what their tongues say).

["For the love of money is a root of all kinds of evil. Some people, eager for money, have wandered from the faith and pierced themselves with many griefs." (1 Timothy 6:10)]

It is again at this point of death that the 'rich man' is identified by the Greek word "*plusios*," as Jesus said, "Died next **kai** this *plusios* **kai** was buried." The same words identify what appears to be an unnamed entity that bears the same name as everyone who serves the god of abundance, who the Romans called Pluto. It becomes important to read "*plusios* " as one would read "*mamónas*,' where the lower case reflects the inferiority of the god they are named after.

Thus, Jesus said, "Died next * this servant of abundance * was buried (i.e.: placed in the ground and covered with earth)."

This is then a powerful statement about the god of the underworld. *Hades*, according to the Greeks, hated those who attempted to escape the eternity of his unseen realm. *Hades* would find those who escaped to the surface and bring them back. The god of the Underworld is why it is so poetically stated "ashes to ashes, dust to dust" during funeral rites. The human body is said to now be worth one U.S. dollar, based on the breakdown of elements it contains. As little as that is worth in currency, you still cannot take anything you own with you when you die.

The Greek name of the god of the underworld is *Hades*, whose name means "the Unseen." The Greeks paid as little attention as possible on this god, whom they loathed. Their ignorance, countered by the Roman's adoration of Pluto as a god of abundance from within the earth (i.e.: iron, salt, gold, silver, copper, tin, etc.) left the name *Hades* relegated to being the name of the realm he ruled. The Underworld became synonymous with Hades.

[Although there is no Hebrew or Israelite mythology, the equivalent master of the Underworld would be the fallen angel that was cast within the Earth for going against God. There is the name *Azazel*, one of the fallen angels written of by Enoch, but Christians prefer the name Lucifer or Satan. Some Hebrews spoke of Beelzebub. They all share common threads with *Hades* and Pluto.]

By understanding this mythological 'history', then see how Jesus said one who worshipped Pluto in life died and was promptly placed back into the earth (interment underground, either placed in a tomb hewn into rock, or laid in a six foot deep hole dug into soil), as the rightful property of his god. Jesus said next (in verse 23), "***kai en tō hadē***," which very capably states, "***kai*** in the realm of the one Hades." [Notice how "*hadē*" is written in the lower case, but loves to be capitalized in translation?]

Neither "*plusios*" nor "*hadē*" is given the respect of capitalization, because those 'proper names' are worthy of lower case identification (as lesser gods); but the lesson of Jesus here is: All who worship Pluto (the god of abundance, wealth, riches, and opulence) will find their souls going to Hell (Pluto's realm), where their god *Hades* reigns. This is regardless of what came out of their mouths when in the flesh, which made them "certain" as believers in Yahweh.

When the one identified as Lazarus died, his body of flesh was not carried by angles to the bosom of Abraham. His flesh was returned to the earth (give unto Pluto what is Pluto's). The burial of his flesh is inconsequential, as his flesh had no value to him, nor anyone "God Has Helped." It was the soul of one whom "God Has Helped" that spiritual messengers lifted away. The implication is that Lazarus lived in the spiritual realm while trapped in his body, having sacrificed his life in the flesh to serve God [like an Apostle or Saint]. This makes Lazarus like the Lazarus Jesus raised (his brother-in-law), who was then another soul living in the spiritual realm within a body of flesh that had been sacrificed to serve the Lord. When Jesus was resurrected, he too was a living Spirit in a dead and worthless body of flesh.

That identifies all who serve Yahweh in the flesh and suffer momentarily (twenty to sixty human years are like a split second in eternity) from the disrespect of the souls whose worship of Pluto (a.k.a. Mammon), who are treated as 'second class' or 'lepers' of society, as being "named Lazarus." All who earn that name, especially those reborn in the name of Jesus Christ, are quite capable of withstanding the suffering of a material world, where the lures of riches no longer are appealing to them. They abstain from taking any more than is necessary to serve Yahweh with strength, meaning they refuse to sell their souls for temporary comfort.

[Joseph of Arimathea was a "rich man," but he used his wealth to support God's ministry in Jesus. He did not love money; he loved Yahweh. God rewarded him with money to use supporting God's Apostles. Had he given all his wealth to those in the name of Jesus Christ, then God would know to trust him with renewed wealth, as an eternal flow of living waters flowing from the earth. This would be as opposed to the efforts required to dig riches from the Underworld.]

The soul of the "rich man" is immediately found unable to withstand an existence that has discomfort, to the point of torment. Fresh from a life in the flesh, where those like Lazarus saw his pretence of royalty and felt the finery of his imported clothing, that soul called out for his fellow "certain man" to serve him with a drop of water placed on the tip of his burning tongue. His soul was so used to living a life of decadence to the max, once removed from a physical body it screamed out for pity, when his former ears ignored the pleas for help that other living beings made to him daily. The karmic reward is shown as being that souls who worship lesser gods in the flesh will find no relief for their souls once removed from that flesh.

In this exchange we read, "So ["*plousios*"] called to him, 'Father Abraham, have pity on me and send Lazarus to dip the tip of his finger in water and cool my tongue, because I am in agony in this fire.'" Here, it is important to see how the rich man in the flesh [who retains the title of *plousios* is the realm of *Hades*] appears to know the name of a poor beggar who had been covered in sores. In the world with a human life the wealthy man [a man of Temple advantages] would have been forbidden by their interpretations of the Law to go near anyone so obviously in a leprous physical condition, meaning it is quite doubtful that one rich man would know the name of a beggar, whose body was full of sores. His calling out "*Lazaron*" [not "*Lazaros*"] says he saw the meaning behind the name, as he was calling out in paid, as one God was punishing, to "the one God Has Helped."

Further, when the translation says "he called," the Greek word written, "*phōnēsas*," better states, "he crowed" or "he cried out loudly." To then say in a loud voice, "have pity on me and send the one God has helped," this is not a prayer of repentance, but a command made by still thinking his having once possessed worldly wealth gave him the power to demand services. By seeing that wicked soul specifically addressed "*Pater Abraam*," the capitalization of "*Pater*" says that wicked soul knew it was speaking to Yahweh, the Father, with the proper name "*Abraam*" being recognition that Yahweh was "the progenitor of the Hebrew race." (Strong's) This is then the wicked soul still believing it was equal to God, as a child of God.

From this realization, God spoke back to the wicked soul, addressing it not as "Son" (the standard translation in most English versions) but as "Child." The Greek word "*Teknon*" is written, which translates as "a child (of either sex)" (Strong's definition), but implies "descendant, inhabitant." (Strong's usage) Thus, the capitalization becomes a statement of importance that says the wicked soul was not a little "child," but was a "Descendant" of Jacob-Israel, making his soul be identified clearly as a "Child" of God.

After that address, God spoke (as *Abraam*, the Father of Israel) to the wicked soul, saying, "remember that in your lifetime you received your good things, while Lazarus received bad things, but now he is comforted here and you are in agony." In the Greek text, the word translated as "while" above is actually one of those ", *kaí*" placements are found, putting emphasis on the polarity that existed in the "lives" (from the Greek word "*zōē*") spent in two bodies of flesh. The wicked soul got all that he sold his soul for **and** "the one God Has Helped" withstood all the "bad" and "evil" (from the Greek word "*kaka*") that the world had to offer for his not bowing down before material riches. The reverse is the promise of the spiritual realm, where comfort, consolation and encouragement (from the Greek word "*parakaleó*") are the rewards of faith and torment, pain and mental anguish (from the Greek word "*odunaó*") are the costs for lack of faith.

Then God spoke as the Father of His people to the one devoted his life to *Hades*, not YHWH, saying: "And besides all this, between us and you a great chasm has been set in place, so that those who want to go from here to you cannot, nor can anyone cross over from there to us.'" Here, the key focus in the Greek has to be on "between us and you," where the Greek text shows "between us *kai* you," which is important to understand, based on the separation created by

Parables Explained: The Parable of the Rich Man & Lazarus

"*kai*."

The Greek word "*metaxy*" is translated as "between," which is an accurate translation. Still, according to Strong's usage, the word means "meanwhile, afterwards," with Thayer's Greek Lexicon adding: "in the mean time." Seeing this difference as a word stating the time beyond the life of a soul in flesh, as the afterlife, the importance of "*kai*" following "us" points to those ("us") who are "the ones God Has Helped," with an absence of the presence of the wicked soul ("you").

Following the "*kai*" is the separate statement that says, "you a chasm great has been fixed." This then says that God has not created a deep rift that physically separates Heaven and Hell; but rather, it is within the souls of the wicked that an impossible gap ("great chasm") "has been fixed." The Greek word "*stérizó*" (the root for "*estēriktai*") says that the rich man (all "*plousios*") "fixed firmly, direct himself towards," and "supported, established and strengthened" (from Strong's usage) this separation "between" himself and God's Kingdom.

Verses twenty-seven and twenty-eight then have "*plousios*" still trying to be an equal to the Father, but continuing to make demand: if not that, then do this. The NIV states him saying, "Then I beg you, father, send Lazarus to my family, for I have five brothers. Let him warn them, so that they will not also come to this place of torment.'" This translation makes some element be exposed that show the audacity of the wicked soul of the "rich man," but the Greek text exposes more that should be realized.

First, to read, "Then I beg you," as what is missed is the

capitalization of "*Erōtō*," which means, "I request, make a request to, pray." (Strong's) The capitalization emphasizes the "**I**" of the deceased (as in the first person singular present active indicative). While begging can be read as the use of this word, the capitalization takes away from any sincerity of pleading with God and turns the verb into a facetious act, like, "Oh yeah. How about if I say 'please'?" It speaks from a past that never prayed seriously to Yahweh, therefore never knowing how prayers are truly answered.

Evidence of this sense of equality comes next, when the written text makes "*pater*" a one-word statement, surrounded by comma marks. The lower-case spelling of "father" diminishes the entity of God, after having pronounced himself as "**I**." This is then furthered by offering the suggestion ("*pempsēs*" in the subjunctive mood), "you would send him" or "you could permit him," with the audacity of thinking God would send Lazarus to his "father" ("*patros*"). The implication is an earthly "father" was more important to the "rich man" than God.

As to the "house" (from the Greek word "*oikon*"), Strong's usage says this word can indicate "a house, the material building; a household, family, lineage, nation." As a wicked soul communicating to God (as the Father of Israel), a request to go to a physical house becomes too limited. The use of "*oikon*" is then a statement about all that the "rich man" valued in the material realm, which would have been his lineage ("house" is akin to a Tribe of Israel ancestry), the organization that sought to secure a sanctuary for self-worship ("house" is akin to Herod's Temple), and especially his cohorts that had a long-range goal of securing a lost land as once again their own nation ("house" is akin to the

Parables Explained: The Parable of the Rich Man & Lazarus

unified Israel of King David).

This is where the realization that "certain men" were known Jews, related as "brothers" in the sense that both (all of their kind) worshiped YHWH, the One God. In the Greek text presentation by BibleHub.com, in their Interlinear Bible presentation of Luke 16, this statement by the "rich man" is separated by double dashes (each called an em dash, em rule or mutton). This, as all placements of punctuation in Scripture, is important to recognize, as the NIV translation obliterates this use of special marks.

A Wikipedia article on em dash states of its usage, "Primarily in places where a set of parentheses or a colon might otherwise be used, it can show an abrupt change in thought or be used where a full stop (period) is too strong and a comma too weak. Em dashes are also used to set off summaries or definitions."

By realizing that intention of this mark that surrounds the text that says "– I have for five brothers – " (rather than ", for I have five brothers.") this identifies an abrupt change in thought as being more strongly emphasized than it would be if set off by a comma mark and a period mark. This importantly repeat the first person voice, saying "**I** have," where the Greek word "*echō*" places great important of what the wicked soul perceives as "his" to hold and possess, beyond material things left behind in the world passed from. Having set this abrupt change of thought up by the pretence of prayer, the wicked soul is now making a demand to God as this being his right as a child of Jacob.

This statement also becomes a pronounced clarification of the "house" of the "father" of "*plousios*," where "five" is an important symbolic number, relative to that right to demand a prayer be answered by Yahweh. According to HELPS Word-studies, the Greek word "*pente*," which clearly translates as "five," can be read symbolically, as "also used in Scripture with added symbolic meaning ("redemption by grace"). They then add (in brackets), "This is derived from the collocations (associations) that "five" has when used in reference to the Tabernacle, Temple, etc."

When esoteric meaning is applied to the number "five," a simple search on Google shows: "The number 5 is commonly referred to as the number of humanity. Human beings have five fingers, five toes, five appendages (if the head is included), five senses, and five major systems of the body. She [I assume a number is referred to here in the feminine] is noted for independence, versatility, rebellion, and a daring nature." In numerology, the number has an association with "divine grace," with it being one-half of ten, where "five" is representative of the human-worldly state of being, seeking God's helping hand to be complete.

Still, while "five" is set apart in verbiage, the unwritten implication is the wicked soul was the sixth "brother" of the earthly father that represented the land. When this is seen and "house" is akin to the House of David, six then reflects the Star of David, which is the symbol of the State of Israel. It is not an a Jewish identification, but it was adopted by Zionists. The six-pointed star is a hexagram, which has been called the "Seal of Solomon." This association to the Temple (as the number "five" implying six) should then be realized as the "house of the father" and the "brothers" therein.

The Greek word "*adelphous*" states "brothers," but brings

out the metaphor of "a brother, member of the same religious community, especially a fellow-Christian." (Strong's usage) While it is easy to get lost in the concept of the old days, when men ran the world, unlike today with the pretence of equality and women's rights having become the philosophy of modern churches, one has to grasp that this use of "brothers" is an emphasized expectation of the wicked soul. The concept of "brothers" is wrong and has to garner more than passing thought of understanding.

First of all, in the context of this parable, where one "certain man" name Lazarus was outcast by another "certain man" ("*plousios*"), the commonality of their religious beliefs (in the One God Yahweh) was not a statement that the two were "brothers." Lazarus was seen (in human life) as a servant to the wealthy, therefore a slave who ran errands for them and nothing more. The wicked soul was demanding services of favor to a brotherhood of wealth and power, with no desire from that spiritual realm of pain and suffering to help the poor of the earth, like Lazarus had been. Thus, "brothers" is a statement of selfishness.

Second,"brother" (the Greek word "*adelphos*") is a masculine noun, making it exclusive of those of the female gender. This goes beyond simply reflecting the ancient ways of male superiority and female submission to that male dominance, to show a lack of recognition that God worked through women (sisters) equally. By the wicked soul being specific of "brothers" and not sisters, that soul knew spiritually how its own incarnations into human flesh was most beneficial in a male body. This, again, is a sign of selfishness.

Finally, the lower-case spelling of "*adelphos*" is an affirmation that the wicked soul knew nothing of the Holy Spirit. When the Apostles wrote of "brethren" (also in the lower-case), it was with the realization of direct relationship with God, from having submitted totally to His Will and becoming reborn as Jesus Christ. God the Father is a masculine entity of spirituality (or positive charged), with the flesh of the earth (clay or dust) being feminine physicality (or negative charged), such the two opposites compliment one another. The fact that physical flesh is divided into male and female bodies is only for the purpose of reproduction, where a man cleaves with a woman and has children. Since this means there is no sexual distinction in the heavenly realm, simply because there is no need to reproduce, the parallel symbolism means that all souls come from God and are thus masculine in nature, placed in feminine (earthly) forms. This makes all souls be related as "brothers" of God, even when those souls are in bodies of flesh that demand human gender distinction. This is a most important concept to grasp.

When an Apostle is said to be "in the name of Jesus Christ," this is not a simple statement that they follow Jesus as those who believe he was the Son of God. It means they have died of self-will and become filled with the Holy Spirit of God, having been resurrected as His Son, Jesus. Spiritually, being possessed by Jesus Christ makes all Apostles (both males and females) be "brothers," simply because they cease being defined by their human sex organs and totally are identified by their masculine souls being combined with the masculine Christ Mind (sent from God) and the masculine face of Jesus they then follow. This makes all Apostles "Brothers," with "brother" and "sister" simply being human gender titles.

Parables Explained: The Parable of the Rich Man & Lazarus

The wicked souls statement, which emphatically broke from a line of thought (marked by two em dashes), to state possession ("I have"), in human form (the symbolism of "five"), where "brothers" are those related to the sins of a wicked soul, *"pente adelphos"* must be read as an emphasis being made on "physical relations." The prayer (demand) should then be read as not a possession of spiritual direction, but one of bloodline worship. His prayer is to feel important again in the worldly realm as an extension of what he had been.

In today's world there is much made about genetic testing for bloodline purposes. Some people wish to find evidence of some exclusive, even royal lineage that shows the querent as special. This should be how to read the impact of "five brothers" is intended to have. The wicked soul saw his bloodline, which was of some Tribe of Israel and some distinction within the tribe of Jerusalem (scribe, Pharisee, Sadducee, High Priest, whatever), as equal to (if not greater than) the brotherhood Jesus was bringing into the world. To serve God Almighty one must not be concerned with how far removed one is to dead relatives (a soul can interchange between such families and is not linked to such past family trees) and be more concerned with how far removed oneself is from God in a world that only leads to death without God.

Following the em dash after *"adelphos,"* the wicked soul returned to its prayerful demands of the soul of Lazarus. We read in the NIV, "Let him warn them, so that they will not also come to this place of torment." Here, the translation is accurate, in particular with the placement of the comma mark kept true to the Greek text. The only caveat being that the translation that says "let him warn," from the

Greek word "*diamartyrētai*," makes better sense when understood as a plea to "let him testify solemnly" or "let him give solemn evidence." (Strong's)

The impact of this root word being a demand to have the spirit of Lazarus "bear witness" to those left behind, still living in the same manner as had the "rich man," speaks loudly as a warning that there is an afterlife. When one sees how Thayer's Greek Lexicon states the root word "*diamarturomai*" has the intent in usage as "religiously to charge," the wicked soul was demanding that proof of an afterlife, especially one that had a "place of torture" or "torment" (from "*toupon touton tēs basanou*"). That speaks of the philosophical differences held between the "brothers."

The word "*basanou*" translates as "torture, torment, examination by torture" (Strong's usage), but it equally represents "a touchstone," which was used to test metals, especially silver and gold. The stone was black in color and could take high heat in the testing of metals. Still, Thayer's Greek Lexicon says one usage (b) was as "the rack or instrument of torture by which one is forced to divulge the truth." This means the usage here, spoken by the wicked soul, is speaking from personally being tested in high heat and found to be impure and worthless. This means the word "*basanou*" is synonymous with the concept of Hell or Hades [more proof that "*plousios*" is associated with worship of the underworld].

Understanding this makes one realize the constant struggle all religions face, especially Judaism and Christianity, where many will talk about an afterlife, with few actually believing one exists. The movement away from religions like the denominations of Christianity is the old Fire and

Parables Explained: The Parable of the Rich Man & Lazarus

Brimstone sermons wore thin, to be replaced by funeral rite words that make it appear even the most wicked human beings are promised heaven by Jesus. The wicked soul in this parable has found the truth [a truth known by God, shared with His Son] of a hellacious afterlife and demands that truth be known by his relatives [not the poor Jews they made a living from].

God then answered the wicked soul's demand offered as a prayer by saying, "They have Moses and the Prophets; let them listen to them." This seems, at first, to be a fairly straight-forward parent-to-child explanation, saying in effect: "No, you will not get your way and here is why ...." That should be grasped, but there are some important subtleties that are missed from this translation from the NIV.

First of all, the Greek word "*Echousi*" is translated as "They have," but that misses the importance of capitalization. This is a direct response to the wicked soul's demand that reached a climax, when the first em dash had the former "rich man" proclaim "**I** have" (from the Greek word "*echō*"). The capitalization addresses how *Abraam* (God the Father of the Jews, as their being ancestors of Abraham) recognizes this sense of the ruling class of Jews thinking they possess God, enough to make demands of Him. With the wicked soul then being a clear possession of God, sentenced to an eternal punishment the "rich man" had no belief in prior, the capitalization places emphasis on "They" and what "They have." God explained that "They have Moses."

Following the proper name "Moses" is the word "*kai*," which introduces a pause that forces one to look closer at the meaning of "Moses." The name (as with all names) is rooted in a word with meaning. Beyond the name being initially Egyptian words that meant "saved from drowning in water," the Hebrew words "*masha*" and "*mashe*" and the Greek word "*muso*" have to be grasped as the importance that comes through capitalization here.

According to the Abarim Publications website of Biblical name meanings, the Hebrew and Greek roots words for "Moses" mean: "*masha*" – "to extract from water"; "*mashe*" – "a loan"; and "*muso*" – "to hide or cover."

All of this meaning must be realized as God's plan in the naming of "Moses," such that the Torah (the "five" books that are the foundation of the Jewish religion) are written in possession of everything that can be deemed as proof of an afterlife. The meaning of the Word must be "extracted" through the emotions that are representative of "water." The Word is "a loan" from God, not something possessed by the people, although it is freely given to them to be led by. Finally, the name "Moses" becomes a statement that the proof of the Word is "hidden and covered" on purpose by God, such that the only way the truth of proof can be exposed is through God sending the Holy Spirit (baptism by Spiritual water) of understanding. Thus, simply by God saying, "They have Moses," He said all the proof "They" need is already in the scrolls "They" read each Sabbath.

Following the "*kai*," is written in Greek, "*tous prophētas*." Rather than hearing God (as Father Abraham) saying there is both "Moses and the Prophets," the "*kai*" separates one from the other, making the second be important to grasp, relative to the first. As such, "Moses" had given all "They" needed, but to help them uncover the hidden meaning a little better, God had also spoken through "the prophets."

There is no capitalization of "*prophētas*," meaning there is no need to bow down and worship holy men, because God speaks through them as He did through Moses. All human beings of true faith becomes "the prophets" of God, through their receipt of God's Holy Spirit.

This understanding then makes the statement following a comma mark, "let them listen to them," be more that this translation allows one to see. The Greek text literally translates to say, "let them hear" (from "*akousatōsan*") "them" (from "*autōn*"). This repetition of "them" [the third person plural aorist imperative verb and the third person plural pronoun] is not so much limited to "them" – "Moses and the Prophets" – but a response to "They," who "have" the scrolls. It is "They" who need to "hear, listen, and comprehend by hearing" (Strong's usage of "*akouó*") what God stated in the Word, by being **them**selves "prophets" of the Lord. After all, they are the ones who get rich from reading the Word aloud. "Let them listen" to what "They" are saying.

This is imperative to grasp firmly, as the wicked soul was demanding that the one "God Has Helped" be sent to "witness" or "warn" his relatives in the Temple of Jerusalem. God, speaking as Abraam, said, "I sent the prophets to warn them and look what happened. 'They' ignored those who were inspired by the Holy Spirit and lost their coveted lands." After those messengers were disregarded, what would the soul of a poor man, outcast from the Temple courts, possible say that "They" would hear?

The aspect of the scribes (who wrote interpretations of the Law), the Sadducees (who did not believe in an afterlife), and the Pharisees (who believed in Sheol as a place for souls to casually wait for the coming of the Son of God) not being able to discern the truth from Scripture was Jesus using parable to point out the lack of true faith "They" had. Jesus constantly confronted them when they attempted to subvert his teachings of the truth, failing miserably. It is vital to see that the failures then, causing this parable to be told as a reflection on that inadequacy, is just as viable today. The lessons taught here in this writing are not the lessons commonly taught by priests, pastors, ministers, or preachers of Christianity. The same absence of the Holy Spirit in those who teach the meaning of God's Word means there is nothing emotionally extracted from the readings from the Holy Bible, which exposes the deeper truth. There is still a common lack in this regard, for the leaders of Christianity to be true prophets of the Lord.

That rejection, both then and now, has to be seen as reflecting in the wicked soul's response to God the Father (speaking as Abraam). We read his reaction to that guidance as: "'No, father Abraham,' he said, 'but if someone from the dead goes to them, they will repent.'" This clearly states the essence of what the wicked soul said, but it misses the finer points that make this seemingly simple statement of ignorance be a profound statement that explains why priests, both then and now, fail to be filled with God's Holy Spirit and serve the Lord completely, speaking the truth as His prophets.

The capitalized Greek word "*Ouchi*," meaning "No," is set apart by comma marks, making it a capitalized one-word statement. The word means, "by no means, not at all" (Strong's usage), but HELPS Word-studies says the word "*ouxi*" is "an emphatic negative adverb, intensifying "*ou*," "not." That source then adds that its usage should be read as "properly definitely not, absolutely out of the question!" There, an exclamation point is the implication of its use. Therefore, the wicked soul was not simply countering what God had told it; it was telling God how that was "Not" good enough and "Not" the way the wicked soul demanded things be done.

Following that absolute rejection, as an expression of equality as a deity, the wicked soul confirmed that it knew to whom it spoke. Again separated by comma marks are the Greek words "*pater Abraam*," of "father Abraham." Because the word "*pater*" is not capitalized, the wicked soul was diminishing God the Father of Israel through Abraham, as just "father Abraham," which says the wicked soul saw itself as a child of a patriarch, but this child was up with the current trends of time and "father Abraham" was out of sync with the way thing were then done. It says the wicked soul spoke to God the Father as a disobedient child, telling its parent what it demands to be done.

After this temper tantrum exclamation, the wicked soul then used logic or reason to hypothesize an "If-Then" scenario. Simply by stating "if" (from the Greek word "*ean*"), following the word of exception, "but" (from the Greek word "*alla*," also meaning "otherwise, on the other hand, and however") the child in this scenario is attempting to pit its brain-power against the All-Knowing Mind of God. It is this love of individual intelligence that makes so many 'smart Christians' bow down before themselves and worship themselves as gods, refusing to accept the Holy Spirit's guidance, without argument.

Here, the wicked soul's reasoning concluded that "they will repent" (from the Greek word "*metanoēsousin*," in the third person future active indicative form). This was his brain-power attempting to see the future through reason and logic, as a deduction for what the result would be, "if one from [the] dead should go to them."

It is important to see the irony of that hypothesis, in two ways. First, Moses and the prophets had been sent a Spirit that clearly (to them) was evidence that repentance was the only way to heaven. The Holy Spirit comes from a life source, however; not a source of death – Earth. That means repentance can never be motivated by any material object, be it person, place or thing. Second, the irony is that Jesus would become like a "corpse" (a viable translation of the Greek word "*nekrōn*"), when he rose from death and walked among his disciples, with the wounds of punishment still fresh on his body. However, the disciples were not led to become Apostles because they saw Jesus as a dead body coming to appear before them, warning them to repent, but because they saw the life of God's Christ prophesying the truth to them. Repentance can only come from receiving the Holy Spirit.

It was at this point that Jesus ended his parable, having God tell the wicked soul, "If they do not listen to Moses and the Prophets, they will not be convinced even if someone rises from the dead." Here, the NIV translation again makes it easy to miss the subtleties of this divine utterance.

First of all, God responded to the brain-power reasoning of the wicked soul, but responding with the divine logic of the Godhead. Here, the capitalized Greek word "*Ei*" is written, translating as "If," which acts as an important correction to the hypothesis "if" offered (from "*ean*"), relative to repentance being the conclusion. The response word can better translate as "Forasmuch as" or an emphasis on "That," which was the erroneous scenario proposed. This means God was rejecting the logic set forth by the wicked soul, "Forasmuch as" it was based on a faulty premise.

God then repeated what He had said before, where the actual statement is "Moses *kai* the prophets." Everything necessary to motivate anyone to repentance is already on "Loan" (from the Hebrew root "*moshe*") to them. Certainly, the verbiage of Moses' Torah (the Word) is deep, with hidden meaning that is covered over (from the Hebrew root word "*mosha*") by ordinary people attempting to paraphrase and swiftly read and discern to suit personal agendas. However, that can be corrected by "the prophets."

God said, "If they will not listen to the divine messengers that I have already sent, then they will not be persuaded (from the Greek word "*peisthēsontai*") **if** (repeating the word "*ean*") one out of a dead body should rise." By repeating the words of the wicked soul, God was speaking not from logic or deductive reasoning, but from His omniscience. God knew that His Son would do just as the wicked soul asked; but the Temple rulers would plot to cover up that appearance and reject it as rebellious fanatics, who were to be said to have stolen a corpse to make it look like it rose from death. Therefore, the conclusion was wrong, as that "if" did not bring about the "then repentance."

The lesson of this parable is then one that speaks of everything one needs to serve the Lord. That need is Spiritual, not material. This is repeatedly written in the Holy texts. This lesson by Jesus is another in a long line of lessons that repeatedly say, "Love the Lord with all your heart, all you soul, and all your mind." Not only do we have Moses *kai* the prophets *kai* Israelite history *kai* the Saints of the New Testament to read and hear the truth come to us via the Holy Spirit, but there is even a Charles Dickens novel that tells the rich to be warned against selfishness. In that parable three ghosts made successful appearances that gained repentance.

The problem now is, as it has always been, the souls who pray to "god" for wealth and get it will always make the mistake of thinking the "god" they prayed to was Yahweh. The sad reality is they are praying to Pluto; and Pluto will pay any price in material goods, knowing nothing material will ever be lost from this world. *Hades* is a hateful god that has claims on every soul in the flesh; and the only way to escape his realm is through Jesus Christ. Then one's soul will be carried away to eternal bliss by angels.

# Parables Explained: The Parable of the Rich Man & Lazarus

Conclusion

The three parables discerned in this book are easily three of the most recognizable parables told by Jesus. The reason is they are very easily popularized as children's stories. For children to remember the imagery presented by Jesus, which were each lessons that were presented to adult men (disciples and/or the Temple elite), the 'moral of the stories' have to be simplified. That simplification is thus what adult Christians remember, and nothing more.

The lesson to love an enemy is easy to say. The application of that in a real world is not so easy to accomplish. Love is one of those physical emotions that changes with the times surrounding one. Most people equate the word "love" with romance and embracing; but what about the love shown by a parent to a child that becomes a lesson: This is going to hurt me more than it hurts you. Few people realize that an enemy is as natural as a friend. If one clearly exists, then so does the other; nary the two shall meet.

The lesson of a good Samaritan says to help everyone in need; but forgets how the application of that lesson in real life has backfired. The result of good helpers being punished because they were sued for not being professional helpers has brought about the need for "good Samaritan laws," designed to protect those who help strangers in need. No one realizes that helping others in need is something all children are born to do, which makes a staged act calling for help often be one designed to lure helpers into a trap. Perhaps, that is the reason why a "certain Man" was beaten and robbed and left for dead.

The lesson of the rich man and Lazarus is the one parable that is most fantasy-like, simply because it projects a picture of the afterlife: Heaven and hell are shown as separated by a great abyss, with plenty of heat to make the wicked suffer. The English translations of this parable, especially when told to children (who grown into adult Christians with childish minds), makes Lazarus be too pitiful to root for. To hear the pleas of the rich man go unheeded by Father Abraham seems cruel. While the lesson of this parable can clearly suggest wealth should be distributed fairly to the poor, that lesson is one that certainly is not easy to accomplish, making this parable appear to be little more than wishful thinking.

The lesson of the prodigal son is another that is easy to remember only the part that deals with one son who was lost and then found. The problem becomes realizing the role of the other son, the elder son, who is the one Jesus told this parable for others to reflect upon. No one calls this The Parable of the Failed Church of God, but that is who the elder son projects. Still, the story is so easily taught to sinners for impact. All human beings know the taste of self-values, which always come with the sacrifice of one's divine inheritance (the innocence of childhood); but, more often than not, real life does not always lead to one eating out of hog troughs for survival. While a promise of redemption is easily taught from this parable, it is the realization of that promise that so many fail to reach.

It should be grasped how Mosaic Law was likewise just as easy to read, but most difficult to live up to that high standard. God sent Jesus to point that out and make equally difficult commands to follow. These parables told in Luke's Gospel are a reflection on how following the Law is not as easy as learning what the Law says. That is where the deeper inspection of what Jesus said becomes the answer to all questions.

By seeing Jesus in the stories he told: as the way to love enemies; as the "certain Man" that was only "half dead"; as Lazarus who was seen as a plight on the Temple and kicked out; and as the "prodigal son" that was not a sinner after all, one can see the truth of obedience to the Law is found in becoming Jesus reborn. By seeing Jesus in these parables, one should hear the call to become the central character of the stories that Jesus told, putting onself in the place of metaphorical Jesus. While that seems as difficult as obeying Laws that are largely unexplained, the answer is only realized by being reborn as Jesus.

Because Jesus was just as human as you and I, he had the same physical, emotional, and spiritual limitations that are placed on all human beings. While it is not written about, Jesus had all the natural urges that come upon every body of breathing flesh. The difference is Jesus was born filled with the Holy Spirit, meaning all human urges were experienced in moderation, simply for the need to realize the strength of human urges. Human urges can only truly be resisted by one removing the "I" from the equation, because "I" stands alone and is easily manipulated. "I" has to be replaced by God and that means the presence of the Christ Mind (the Mind of God, sent as His Holy Spirit). Jesus was born with that Mind, as promised by God to be greater than any Israelite brain ever. Thus, Jesus could resist all urges to sin by facing them and commanding them to get behind him.

To see Jesus as the only one ever to be able to resist all urges to sin belittles the purpose of God to promise eternal salvation to come to His faithful, through the promise of the Son (a Messiah). To see Jesus as an equal to God belittles God. The first Commandment says any other gods shall never stand before the face of God; that means worshiping Jesus as a god is forbidden by YHWH.

Jesus repeatedly said that he did not speak for himself, but for the Father. When Jesus added, "Believe me when I say that I am in the Father and the Father is in me" (John 14:11a), Jesus said all of his glory was from God. When Jesus then went further, saying "at least believe on the evidence of the works themselves," (John 14:11b), which says every act of Jesus, including his ability to resist the urges of sin, was due to God totally leading his being.

God said through the prophets [Ezekiel and Jeremiah], "I will put my law within them, and I will write it on their hearts. And I will be their God, and they shall be my people." (Jeremiah 31:33b) Jesus was the prototype that was sent to bring about that new covenant with the children of Israel. As the prototype, Jesus is the Spiritual King of all who will devote their lives to the Lord. As the King, each true Christian will sacrifice themselves (their self-egos of human will), making their flesh (each human body submitting its life to God) become the Kingdom of God. Jesus is the King that lead a soul (its body of flesh following) to the eternal kingdom.

When that lordship is freely given and one has married one's soul with God, through a baptism by the Holy Spirit, then Jesus will be King over one's being. The blood of Christ will pump figuratively through one's veins and arteries, pumped by the heart of flesh that sends the laws of God to every cell in the body. The blood reaches the flesh of a human brain and transforms it Spiritually to the Christ Mind, so all physical sensations that are to sin are no longer effective. This is then the only way one can truly be Christian and be guaranteed eternal life.

The deeper story that is contained in the Greek of Luke, including his use of punctuation, says Jesus spoke in parables about how one acts when the laws of God are written on one's heart of flesh. One loves by a willingness to let a world that loves sin to sin. God's Love is the only driving purpose in a committed wife's subjection to her Husband (with all human beings of all genders meant to be brides of God). One helps others who are likewise married to God, thus Jesus' other resurrections as true Christians, and true Christians always help other true Christians, while also being the model of Jesus for those seeking the truth. That is the true meaning of Christianity, as Christianity is a brotherhood (brothers and sisters reborn as the Son of God) that equates to true neighbors.

One filled with the Holy Spirit and reborn as Jesus Christ will abstain from the lures of the material world, which is most commonly found creating the rich. Those who live as Jesuses reborn will be seen as diseased and impoverished (as Lazaruses). Only one who totally subjects self to God will never worry about how, when, where, or from whom one's needs will be met. Faith can only be held by those who serve God with complete trust that whatever the future brings, then it will be to meet one's needs. As was seen in the story of Jesus of Nazareth, and as he promised to his disciples, in the same way that the parable of Lazarus is projected, the world will chew one up and spit one out through persecution of those who are in the name of Jesus Christ.

It is my hope and prayer that all who have read this book will read it multiple times. It is not enough to say you believe what I write. You must be able to see what I see with your own eyes. In that way this book is a training exercise, which means repeating until what I am teaching has become owned by the one being taught. Those who say, "If Jesus were here, he would say do this or do that," are proof that the Holy Spirit is not with them. Only the true disciple that has become transformed into an Apostle says what Ezekiel said, when God asked him, "Mortal, can these dry bones live?"

By saying, "You know," one has just confessed to self-sacrifice, admitting that what one thinks is nothing when compared to the Godhead. The lessons of this book are so you will be able to see how great Holy Scripture is. It is so great that one human brain of flesh cannot possibly memorize it all. Therefore, it is best to admit that failure and let God take over one's life.

Robert Tippett

Parables Explained: Conclusion

Robert Tippett

Parables Explained: Conclusion

www.ingramcontent.com/pod-product-compliance
Lightning Source LLC
Chambersburg PA
CBHW020648300426
44112CB00007B/284